Understanding Education

CW00921493

Understanding Educational Expeditions

Simon Beames
University of Edinburgh, UK

SENSE PUBLISHERS
ROTTERDAM/BOSTON/TAIPEI

A C.I.P. record for this book is available from the Library of Congress.

ISBN 978-94-6091-123-1 (paperback)
ISBN 978-94-6091-124-8 (hardback)
ISBN 978-94-6091-125-5 (e-book)

Published by: Sense Publishers,
P.O. Box 21858,
3001 AW Rotterdam,
The Netherlands
http://www.sensepublishers.com

Printed on acid-free paper

Front cover by Stephanie Ryan ("Bear Glacier")

Illustrations by Mary Higgins

All Rights Reserved © 2010 Sense Publishers

No part of this work may be reproduced, stored in a retrieval system, or transmitted in any form or by any means, electronic, mechanical, photocopying, microfilming, recording or otherwise, without written permission from the Publisher, with the exception of any material supplied specifically for the purpose of being entered and executed on a computer system, for exclusive use by the purchaser of the work.

TABLE OF CONTENTS

PREFACE

The fact that you are reading this preface suggests that you are curious about the ways in which expeditions may (or indeed may not) be effectively used for educational purposes. Although individual journal papers and practical "how to" books on expeditions exist, there is no collection of writing that brings together a wide range of theoretical perspectives that can inform real-world practice. This book begins to address this gap in the literature.

Although people have undertaken self-sufficient journeys with a purpose since the beginning of time, the idea of taking others on an expedition that was designed to somehow make them better people is, I believe, rather ambitious and worthy of closer examination. As people in positions of power, we have considerable responsibilities to the participants - often young and vulnerable - with whom we work.

So, who is this book for? It is for university lecturers and students, as well as for expedition providers and leaders. Bridging the theory/practice divide is an essential aspect of the book. To this end, contributors have been encouraged to maintain the rigour of their academic writing, but in a style that is intended to be accessible to a broad audience. Further, each chapter ends with suggested implications for practice. I want practitioners to finish reading a chapter and be able to take away something that they can incorporate into their work. Discussion questions are offered as a means of encouraging critical thinking and debate in classroom or staffroom settings.

As the book took shape, I discovered that the world of educational expeditions is more diverse and complex than I had originally thought. So, by completing the project I have realised that, in fact, it is not complete at all; many other issues and perspectives remain to be examined.

In terms of editing, one universal spell check has not been applied. American contributors have used "program" rather than "programme", British writers have used "colour" rather than "color", and the Canadians – true to their history – are caught somewhere in the middle. There is, admittedly, a British bias in some chapters. Still, I am confident that the majority of the content will be of interest to anyone involved in educational expeditions – whether they take place in familiar settings or overseas.

The book begins with Chris Loynes' examination of the historical and cultural perspectives of educational expeditions. Next are three chapters using philosophical, sociological, and anthropological frameworks to consider expedition practice: Paul Stonehouse writes about applying Aristotelian virtue ethics, I explore the usefulness of interactionist social theory, and Brent Bell, together with Will Carlson and me, examines the potential and pitfalls of drawing on Rites of Passage as a model for designing learning experiences.

The middle section of the book concentrates on expeditions that have additional explicit aims. First, Tim Stott outlines important considerations for groups doing scientific fieldwork. Pete Allison and Kris Von Wald's contribution follows, with their careful treatment of expeditions that have personal, social, and health education as their principle goal. The section is completed by Morten Asfeldt, Glen Hvenegaard, and Ingrid Urberg's insights into expeditions that are an integral part of a university liberal arts programme.

The next section of the book starts with Bob Henderson's reflections on heritage travel and the role of place, story, and technology. This is followed by John Crosbie's deconstruction of the language, assumptions, and issues associated with expeditions for people with disabilities. Andrea Nightingale's examination of the ethics of travelling to, and conducting research in and among, foreign cultures finishes this section.

The book closes with a chapter on current issues written by Pete Allison and me. We highlight six key areas that are not explicitly covered in other chapters: volunteer work; cultural sensitivity and environmental responsibility; psychological considerations; regulating practice; conducting research; and accessibility.

I am amazed by how much I have learned about educational expeditions through putting this book together. In fact, my advice to anyone who would like to learn about a subject is to edit a book about it! This is my segue into thanking the authors for their valuable contributions to this book. I am grateful for the time they took to write chapters so rich in content, as well as for their patience with my pedantic editing.

I thank Mary Higgins for her brilliant cartoons. They serve to ensure that, although we may passionately believe in what we do, we do not take ourselves too seriously. Peter de Liefde, from Sense Publishers, also deserves my thanks, as he agreed to publish a book that he knew would not become a number one best-seller. I am grateful for the time that Frances - my editor-mentor - gave to commenting on the chapters.

Finally, thanks to Nancy for her constant support and encouragement.

SKB
Edinburgh
Autumn 2009

CHRIS LOYNES

1. THE BRITISH YOUTH EXPEDITION: CULTURAL AND HISTORICAL PERSPECTIVES

The UK has a long tradition of expeditions, a strong cultural idea that has become a common element of non-formal education. According to the Young Explorers Trust (Young Explorers Trust, 2009), over 600 youth expeditions leave the UK each year. At home, the Duke of Edinburgh's Award groups, Scouts and Guides, among many other youth organisations, account for innumerable journeys. The expedition idea also contributes towards the UK version of the gap year. The numbers involved increase considerably if recreational trips and their associated informal educational benefits are added to the list.

Expeditions have sea-faring as well as land-based traditions. The Sail Training Association and Ocean Youth Trusts, along with a fleet of other "tall ships" built specifically for youth, take thousands to sea each year. The iconic re-creation of the historical voyages of Drake from 1978–1980 and Raleigh from 1984–1988 have also left a legacy of expeditions, now largely on land, both at home and abroad.

The word "expedition" is important. "Expedition" conjures up something specific that is somehow different from "journey", "trip" "travelling", "touring", "backpacking" or "voyage". It also feels different from related words used in other cultures, such as "wanderlust", "tramping", "trail walking", "walkabout" or "safari". For some, "expedition" implies a wilderness setting. For others, it means contrasting cultures and landscapes.

Whether by land or sea, expeditions have a varied history influenced by politics and religion, economics and empire, science, adventure, and service. The purpose of this chapter is to explore some of these historical and cultural roots and review the ways in which the values attached to them have impacted on the more recent idea of youth expeditions in the UK and other countries. I hope that this review will enable readers to reflect on the underlying values embedded in their own expeditions, whatever the historical and cultural background. Ideally, this should help readers construct values that are more congruent with their aspirations. I was once asked how to make sure that a leader could recruit the right people to an expedition. I replied that I thought that all a good leader had to do was to stand up and shout clearly about his or her ideas and the right people would roll up. This chapter is intended to help with the clarity of that "shout".

People have been travelling for instrumental reasons for a very long time. What has changed over time, and in relation to the cultural trends in society, are the motivations for these journeys. In addition, the nature of human relations both with nature and with other cultures changes as these motivations change. Despite the waves of immigration at various points, archaeologists think that Neolithic times

S. K. Beames (ed.), Understanding Educational Expeditions, 01–15.
© 2010 Sense Publishers. All rights reserved.

were largely peaceful. Settlements were largely undefended and trade widespread. The surrounding landscape did change as a result of human activity, but again, only imperceptibly over thousands of years. It took far more rapid and far-reaching changes in the later stages of British history to shape our current relationships with and impact upon other landscapes and cultures, relationships that are mirrored by our current attitudes to travelling and especially expeditions.

MEDIEVAL THEMES

In Europe, since the establishment of early civilisations in the eastern Mediterranean and beyond, armies and traders have travelled to conquer other settlements or to exchange surpluses of goods. However, for most ordinary people, travel was something you did as a slave or a conscript.

In the early medieval period the Crusades attracted some people to travel for economic gain. However, most commanders had a sense of defending a particular, Christian way of life. Their motivation was ideological. Most soldiers, on the other hand, were ordinary people conscripted, or occasionally, volunteers. While ideas of a life with greater purpose were probably a factor for some, this was less influential than the demands of a lord or the promise of being financially maintained. It is possible that simple curiosity motivated some, at least in part. Whatever the reason, these travels, spread over several centuries of British history, provided a new means for the ordinary person to see beyond their own communities travel. Journeys to exotic places were always a source for good storytelling that probably inspired a constant trickle of the needy, greedy, and curious.

Pilgrimage also has a long tradition that took ordinary people to religious sites throughout the UK and especially into continental Europe. As well as opening up the possibility of travel to the ordinary person, these forms of travel stand out, as they sometimes lacked the utilitarian motive of personal, if not collective, gain.

Throughout Europe another practice maintained the possibility of travel for ordinary men if not for women. In the city-states of central Europe, including, for a time, some English cities, an apprentice had to learn his trade in another city. This built up networks for markets and dispersed new ideas and technologies. The widening of the apprentice's horizons was also thought to be a good thing, offered as a special reward for loyalty and talent. While it can be argued that these are utilitarian motives, there are also elements of personal fulfilment and social mobility contained in the practice. It clearly holds educational intentions. Interestingly, these are also justifications put forward for some modern expeditions. Travel has a long history of enhancing employability and raising social standing.

Wanderlust is a German word for a practice found throughout Europe that is (can omit) built on these concepts. Some states expected young men to leave their homes and make their fortune elsewhere before returning to start families and businesses. Typically the wanderer had to leave penniless, which is a theme that underpins the ever popular "rags to riches" stories, such as Dick Whittington. This theme resonates with tales of gap year experiences both in relation to the penniless state of the traveller (e.g. "you are not a traveller until you no longer have enough money in your pocket or on your credit card to buy a flight home"), and in relation to its transformational potential on the trajectory of the life stories of participants.

EMPIRE

During the sixteenth century, England, based on its sea faring and economic power, began establishing trading links in Asia. The Crown invested in these expeditions in order to fund wars in Europe. Merchants banded together to raise the capital to underwrite a voyage from which great profits were made if the ships returned. Many did not. The concept of venture capital was established and risk, that is, financial risk, was routinely assessed and insured against for the first time. This may be the first time that the assessment of risk was institutionalised on a cost/ benefit basis. While the risk, in this case, was financial, the language and conceptual framework with which risk to people is currently understood in adventure education is based on these same principles.

After a while, captains and trading companies forged alliances with local rulers. Later they usurped them to become the rulers of many of these lands, eventually exporting English institutions and bureaucracies as well as armies. In return, England imported and traded in slaves, raw materials and food - goods that underpinned the farming and industrial revolutions. Despite the involvement of many other European nations, these actions established England as the major world power of the day, and contributed to the nation's sense of cultural, economic, and moral superiority.

Later, a growing population and the growing demand for resources led to the quest for new lands and the establishment of colonies in more "primitive" places such as Australia, New Zealand, and North America. The lands and resources of these places were understood as possessions. Judgements about others were made using the civilisations of Europe as the benchmark. The native people were understood as, at best, primitive, and, at worst, animals to be slaughtered. Missionaries set out to convert these people from their pagan ways. Farmers imposed alien livestock and crops on unsuitable ecosystems, though tobacco, potatoes and corn were adopted from North America. Scientists collected knowledge and specimens from everywhere they could reach so that British museums and institutions possessed the local knowledge as well as the resources (Hanbury-Tenison, 1993). Later, explorers "conquered", mapped, and "summitted" what could not be possessed (Fleming, 2001). In all of these situations, we exported and imposed our culture. At the same time, resources and knowledge were expropriated for our own purposes and with no thought to the needs or rights of the local people (Ellis & Ellis, 2001). Whole peoples and ecosystems were destroyed and other species driven into extinction or rarity.

Undoubtedly, many of the later explorers such as geographers, cartographers, scientists and plant collectors were motivated by curiosity. Nevertheless, they often acted unthinkingly in their relations with local people and wildlife. For example, even Darwin and the crew of the Beagle had a devastating impact on the populations of the giant tortoises of the Galapagos at the very same time as they realised their special nature. Their speciation, only noticed because of the slaughter, even contributed to Darwin's development of the theory of evolution (Taylor, 2008).

It is easy to imagine that such practices have long since ceased. However, a British youth expedition, only two decades ago, was responsible for the desecration of the sacred sites of local people and the destruction of the vegetation of a whole island, with the resultant loss of at least one endemic species. While these outcomes were not intentional they were the result of people assuming they understood a distant culture and environment when they did not.

The violence associated with the establishment of the Empire is no longer a common feature of the British presence in the world, although some would point to the exploitation and oppression of local people and the threats to wildlife and ecosystems by some political and corporate groups for commercial gain as evidence that such practices are far from being outlawed. Others might comment on the motives behind the British involvement in the invasions of Iraq. However, many of the attitudes of the early explorers remain at the heart of the British expedition. Scientists and adventurers still leave the UK to discover new knowledge, visit and map remote places, climb new peaks, descend new rivers, and explore new caves. Others seek to go further/faster/younger in a quest for celebrity in the explorers' halls of fame. There remains a tradition of winning knowledge and conquering places for the nation. Union Jacks are often involved. As illustrated above, concern for the interests or needs of the local people or wildlife are still problematic at times - as is the ownership of the knowledge that is brought back. For example, the British Museum still refuses to return the Elgin marbles looted from Athens by British archaeologists. The Victorian approach to exploration and overall worldview of a superior culture with the right to possess knowledge and experience of other places is still deeply embedded in the rationale for the expedition.

Some institutions have only recently begun to redress these failings. Kew Gardens, the home of one of the world's oldest and most comprehensive herbariums, is digitising its collection to give access to all on line. Likewise, the Royal Geographical Society is digitising its map and photograph collections. Both institutions have been collaborating with scientists from other parts of the world in order to develop knowledge of value to them, such as cataloguing bio-diverse and little-known ecosystems under threat, and tackling local concerns, such as invasive species (Desmond, 2007). These are relatively recent, but heartening trends.

Adventurers still roam the world looking for "firsts". Yet, there are also growing signs of reciprocity. Doug Scott, an experienced Himalayan mountaineer, is, like a growing number of visitors to this region, seeking to give back to the country from which he has gained so much. He leads a charity providing education for remote Nepalese villagers. He also promotes the outstanding achievements of local mountaineers, many of whom have consistently outperformed Europe's best. Yet, unlike their European counterparts, they receive little recognition in their home country or in other countries with mountaineering traditions.

ROMANTIC COUNTER CURRENTS

During the eighteenth century the romantics changed the way in which increasing numbers of people saw wild places and the way they understood endeavours that took place in these landscapes. The awesome and dramatic landscapes were understood to hold transformational power. It was felt that beauty could take people out of their normal and ordinary experiences shocking them into spiritual realisations. These ideas were so radical to society at that time that, in their early years, Wordsworth and Coleridge were spied on by the state. Coleridge (2008) captured the central concept in "The Rime of the Ancient Mariner". After the crew shoot the beautiful albatross the ship is lost. All, but the mariner who tells the story, die. Facing what he believes to be certain death and surrounded by wild and fierce serpents, he finds he is sympathetic to their condition in spite of the threat they pose. Immediately, wind rises and the ship is born back to known waters and the mariner's salvation. Nature, and from the perspective of expeditions, "exotic nature", encountered during an extended journey, restored a sense of higher values and moral purpose in humans. The idea of nature as a repository of a higher sense of self has remained central in outdoor recreation and education ever since, as has the idea of extended travels and expeditions as transformational experiences.

In the seventeenth century, the romantised experience of nature became part of the grand tour – the educational travels of the young of the social elite. This included visits to the Alps alongside cultural immersions in Rome and Athens. Later, when these tours could not go to Europe because of war, the elite travelled to the Lake District and Scotland for their dose of wild and mountainous grandeur and personal transformation (Black, 2003).

A related and later movement was a more socially widespread tourism. Based on the new wealth of the middle classes from the industrial revolution, guide books and tour operators led people to the picturesque and the awful – even into the "jaws of Borrowdale!". Viewpoints were established such as Surprise View in Borrowdale, which overlooks Derwent Water with Skiddaw in the background. The essential element of this view is that it is from the edge of a precipitous cliff which the observer comes upon suddenly after walking through trees. Waterfalls became focal points and were developed with tree plantings, footpaths, and bridges that took people as close to the power and roar of the falling water as possible. Streams were often diverted to add to the power of the fall (Price, 2000).

For both of these social trends the wild came to symbolise something free from civilisation, based on egalitarian and self-reliant ideals. Wordsworth was a fan of the principles of the French revolution, and referred to Cumbria as a "republic of shepherds". This was based on the what he understood to be the independent, egalitarian (yet mutually supportive) lives of the local people as much as on the elements and open landscapes (Bate, 2000). Yet, when the railways began to open up these landscapes to the working classes, Wordsworth expressed concern that such people would not have the appropriate eyes with which to fully appreciate the beauty of the fells. He protested against the railway on these grounds.

The Romantic Movement defined and encouraged a secular pilgrimage to remote places of awesome power and beauty. Mountain tops, viewpoints, waterfalls, headlands, and ancient trees and became the foci of outings. The idea was readily extended to the "tour" and, later, the expedition, as explorers sought out even more remote and challenging mountain tops, waterfalls, poles, and river sources. These excursions became readily commodified and sold in packages to the developing tourism market.

The veneration of nature by the romantics is closely paralleled by a separation from it. The physical separation of a growing percentage of the population through urbanisation led to an increasing demand for opportunities to visit the countryside. In addition, the enlightenment, which saw the world as a laboratory to study, understand, and control, was countered by the emotional and aesthetic approach of the romantic idea. From early on, the tendency for modern culture to separate people from nature was vigorously countered by demands to reconnect with it in new ways, largely in people's growing leisure, rather than work, time (Glyptis, 1991).

The desire to return to the countryside gave birth to a vigorous recreation movement once the growing wealth of the industrial revolution began to trickle down to working class people. People walked and cycled amazing distances in limited time and with little equipment. Even visits to the seaside involved travelling to a space that gave the holidaymakers a sense of freedom, escape, and "a breath of fresh air". These trends would be celebrated today as supporting the health and well-being of an over-urbanised and stressed people. Then, they were understood as an escape from the drudgery and routine of work and urban life, a recreation of the spirit.

A WIDER PERSPECTIVE

While the historical context above is a British one, several themes can be applied to other countries. Many of the values embedded in British history are also the values embedded in much of western civilisation and even the emerging global culture.

However, each time expeditions emerge in a new culture and environment they are, in part, transformed. For example, the push north and west by explorers and traders in North America, while based on European traditions and linked directly to European trade routes, gave rise to new possibilities. The environment encouraged the adoption of new modes of travel. For example, in order to make travel easier through heavily wooded country, winter travel on snowshoes and following river systems in canoes were adopted as ways of journeying. The latter involved constructing and using portage trails - an activity now mysteriously celebrated by recreational canoeists. Less puzzlingly, these routes and activities, together with many of their rituals and traditions, have formed the basis of a different youth expedition culture (see for example Henderson, 2007). Seen this way, specific landscapes and the human history that has shaped them, can underpin rich, culturally-relevant approaches to expedition practice.

It was not just the environment that led to different traditions. The presence of indigenous people led to a range of encounters and transactions that had a strong influence on the European travellers as they explored the "new" country. Some encounters even influenced practices back in the UK. For example, Seton, an early social reformer, established the Woodcraft Folk youth movement, which is based on an admittedly romanticised view of the lives of certain indigenous peoples. He replicated the egalitarian structure of their society and placed a high value on their rituals, and practices such as circle meetings and reciting creeds at their beginning. He also thought the simple life in nature was a central element in the quality of life he was trying to recreate. To this day, the Woodcraft Folk are a camping-based, family organisation with strong values concerning peaceful human relations in camp and around the globe (Smith, 2002).

Paths taken by different cultures can also be illustrated by their respective approaches to outdoor travel guiding. For example, professional qualifications, traditions, and practices for sea kayak coaches (the term is an indication of the focus) in the UK, encourage an experience that emphasises the skills involved in making the journey. Undertaking long passages, tackling rough water, and reaching remote locations, with all the imperial overtones of conquest and achievement, are highlighted. However, on the west coast of Canada, kayak guides are more likely to take their clients "into" an environment. They are trained to interpret the culture and natural history of the place, to camp using "leave no trace" principles, and provide the sufficient skills necessary to explore the area. This approach may have more in common with some forms of leadership on African safaris or Australian bushwalks than with British sea kayak guiding. Readers who are familiar with these different traditions may like to explore what they believe to be the historical and cultural influences that have led to such strong differences in the values they represent.

THE EMERGENCE OF YOUTH EXPEDITIONS

The first expedition specifically for youth took place in the context of a moral panic surrounding the attitudes of working class young people growing up at the end of the Victorian period. This panic was the latest in a series in which the established middle and upper classes expressed concern about the youth of the day - especially the working class youth. Victorian social reformers adopted various approaches as a means of "helping" the working class develop appropriate values in their efforts to become socially mobile. These included workers' education and the emergence of various youth movements, most of which are still in existence today.

Arguably, it was Baden-Powell (widely known as BP), founder of the Boy Scouts in 1907, who led the first ever youth expedition to Brownsea Island - an uninhabited island in Poole Harbour on the south coast of England. Camping and conducting self-reliant journeys in the countryside became established as a core part of the Scout programme from the beginning. BP's military background enabled him to see the potential of using the outdoors for health and moral education. Although he was concerned with preparing young men for war, he also wanted to provide a moral equivalent to war. As a general in the Boer War, he had seen how quickly boys matured into men with a strong sense of moral purpose, self-discipline, and a sense of duty, as well as a wide range of abilities in the context of scouting for the army. The Scout Movement was intended to provide a programme that elicited the same outcomes in a civilian context. It contained many of the elements widely considered to be good practice on youth expeditions, including working in groups (often with a vertical age structure), opportunities for peer leadership, self-reliance, physical fitness, and challenging pursuits. The role of adult leaders was to inspire, motivate, and empower young people to gain a sense of fulfilment through their own achievements. A service ethic was a strong element of the approach and this programme, along with most others developed before the Second World War, can be characterised by asking the question of young people, "what have I got to give to society?" (Smith, 1997b).

Kurt Hahn continued the development of youth expeditions for educational purposes. His innovations have had a profound impact on the style of youth expeditions and their current popularity. Hahn introduced the concept of self-reliant journeys in the mountains as part of a wider experiential approach to secondary education at Gordonstoun, the public school where he was headmaster. Initially, he wished to raise the moral tone of the aspirant ruling elite that, in his view, was threatened by a moral decline in society. He soon saw the potential of his programme for all young people, and developed it for local boys and girls as the Moray Badge Scheme - a programme that led, after the war, to the Duke of Edinburgh's Award Scheme. This programme has probably led more young people into open and wild country in the UK and abroad on self-reliant expeditions than any other. The scheme has also been widely replicated in other countries (Smith, 1997a). Hahn also embedded the expedition into the heart of the Outward Bound programme, which is also widely reproduced in Outward Bound schools around the world. In the early days, many local authorities ran outdoor education centres that followed Hahn's example. Nowadays, however, as programmes have become increasingly shorter in length, expeditions are an unusual feature of most outdoor centres, including Outward Bound.

While this may be the case in the UK, it is not so everywhere. Many Outward Bound Schools around the world (over 40 on six continents according to Outward Bound International) carry out "British style" self-reliant expeditions with apparently little thought to the values that are being reproduced. Various versions and reproductions in other countries (e.g. Scouting, Guiding, and the Duke of Edinburgh's Award Scheme have likewise transported British practices and their underpinning values with little critical thought. It could be argued that this is a good example of British imperialism alive and well. Brookes (2002) makes just this point in relation to the ways in which the Australian environment is explored and understood. It could also be possible that these neo-colonial forms of practice are very good at transmitting and reproducing the dominant values of an increasingly global world. Either way, I would suggest that it is important to identify the values underpinning these practices, and then carefully consider whether they should be reproduced, adapted, or abandoned.

BP and Hahn encouraged self-reliant journeys in remote and unfamiliar country. However, with some exceptions, these journeys took place within the UK. It was another organisation that started the overseas tradition. The Public Schools Exploring Society, now known as the British Schools Exploring Society (BSES), was founded in 1932 by Commander Murray Levick (RN). Levick accompanied Scott on his Antarctic expedition and, on his retirement from the Royal Navy, founded BSES in order to take young men on expeditions to remote and unknown parts of the world. BSES has evolved over the decades into a youth development charity open to all young people regardless of their backgrounds, school, sex or ability. Their current aim is given below.

> BSES Expeditions is a youth development charity which aims to provide young people with inspirational, challenging scientific expeditions to remote, wild environments and so develop their confidence, teamwork, leadership and spirit of adventure and exploration. (British Schools Exploring Society, 2009, para 1)

While BP and Hahn had their roots in the Romantic Movement's ideals of transformative experiences in nature, the underpinning values of BSES were firmly in the imperial traditions of exploration. Knowledge and status were to be won from remote and challenging exploits abroad. Perhaps of all the youth expedition organisations, BSES illustrates how traditions both inspire and influence educational endeavours. They also illustrate vividly how an organisation can reflect these original values by holding on to those that are still considered to be of worth and by abandoning or adapting others.

POST-WAR DEVELOPMENTS

After the Second World War, BSES introduced a new theme into youth development. As prosperity grew and spread through society, more people could aspire to the "good life". People gradually shifted their moral focus from "what can I give to society?" to "what can society give to me?". Expeditions were becoming a vehicle for personal fulfillment, and youth expeditions began to justify their endeavours in terms of the value of adventure for personal development. Among these post-war expedition programmes were the Brathay Exploration Group and Endeavour. Brathay, for example, declared its purpose to be the broadening of the horizons of young working people (Dybeck, 1996).

Endeavour, like BSES, had its roots in imperial traditions, but with a significant element of romanticism added. Their founder was Everest leader John Hunt. He, along with a group of climbers, wanted to make the powerful experiences they had experienced climbing in the Himalaya and elsewhere, available to young people (Cranfield, 2002). They also realised that they knew little about young people and education, so they enlisted the help of a youth leader called Dick Allcock, who was recommended to them by Kurt Hahn. Allcock had been running early versions of the Duke of Edinburgh's Award Scheme. It was he that ensured that the first expedition, to Greenland, was a mixed sex expedition. He also introduced the idea that the young people should select their adult leaders rather than the other way around. In addition, he ensured that science and service were seen as equally important elements of the expedition's purpose as was adventure. The second expedition was to Greece. It involved a trek north through the Pindus Mountains, during which Allcock recognised the significant value of an engagement with another culture. In these ways, Allcock was ahead of his time, as he laid down principles that took decades for the majority of youth expedition organisations to adopt (Allcock, 2002).

Led by volunteers and with strong liberal educational philosophies, these organisations were the precursors to Operation Drake, Operation Raleigh (now Raleigh International) and World Challenge. They were similarly rooted in strong imperial traditions, but tempered both by romantic ideals and liberal educational values. An early emphasis on public school participation soon broke down into a wide range of groups planning and undertaking trips.

EXPEDITIONS AT SEA

Operations Drake and Raleigh were ambitious programmes inspired by the anniversaries of their respective voyages of discovery (Chapman, 1986). Set up by Blashford Schnell, an army officer, they were clearly rooted in the nationalistic values of imperial traditions. Interestingly, the two programmes have contrasting legacies. Young people returning from Operation Drake were charged with starting programmes within the UK that would give access to powerful expedition (and other outdoor) experiences for young people who would not imagine, or could not afford, a Drake voyage. Some of these programmes are running to this day, for example, Venture Scotland. Operation Raleigh, on the other hand, has led to a sustained programme of overseas expeditions in parts of the world where they developed considerable expertise. They currently offer some of the longest and remotest expedition opportunities for young people. Each, like the early Endeavour expeditions, has an environmental, adventure, and service component.

Youth voyages had been taking place for some years before Drake and Raleigh. Two contrasting approaches were started in the fifties and early sixties, and each was based on a different sailing tradition. The Sail Training Association organised long voyages for young people in British waters and further afield on Tall Ships races. McCulloch (2004) highlights the way in which the traditions of command and hierarchical crew structures prevail on board to this day. By contrast, the Ocean Youth Club, now the Ocean Youth Trust, built a fleet of Bermudan sloops and, McCulloch claims, based their approach to sailing and crew management on the more egalitarian traditions of leisure sailing that developed in the early part of the twentieth century. The two styles demonstrate how traditions from the past can be very engrained and persistent. However, like BSES, both organisations have attempted to reinterpret the meanings of the values that underpin their ways of doing things in modern educational terms.

British Trends

Ted Grey (1984), chair of the young Explorers Trust for many years, describes a trend that he has noticed over the 40 years of his career. Grey led school expeditions from the working class areas of the Nottingham coalfield. He notes that early expeditions typically went to cold climates and had a scientific purpose. For example, a major achievement by school expeditions in the sixties and seventies was the mapping of the retreat of glaciers in Iceland, which was masterminded by Tony Escritt and involved many schools over two decades. The results gave one of the earliest indications of global climate change (Escritt, 1985). According to Grey, in the 1970s more and more trips became overt about their adventure aims as this idea gained more educational recognition. For example, Alasdair Kennedy, an inspirational teacher from Liverpool, ran expeditions across the Sahara for 25 years. The trips were the culmination of a year of preparation and training, as an alternative curriculum for truanting students (Kennedy, 1992). From the 1980s and onwards, Grey identified a growing concern for social and environmental issues amongst young people and he claims that youth expeditions increasingly adopted a service approach. The focus has also moved, he claims, from cold and remote places to hot and inhabited ones. By the end of the 1980s, an immersion in another culture had become as common an element of a youth expedition programme as exposure to a contrasting and dramatic landscape.

A EUROPEAN PERSPECTIVE

It is sometimes easier to notice how the approach taken in one country is particular to its history and culture when it is compared with the approaches taken in other countries. Here are two examples that throw British ways of journeying into perspective.

Friluftsliv is the name given across Scandinavia for their versions of outdoor education. In Norway, the concept has grown over the last one hundred years, alongside the development of a young nation. Fostering people's relationships with the land was employed as part of the process of building a sense of national identity. Norwegians tramp and ski through the mountains and fells that run along the spine of the country. In doing so they understand the journey as a way of connecting with the land that represents core beliefs about the nation and the culture. Along with the celebration of old ways of fishing and farming, friluftsliv gives Norwegians a sense of common identity and values. Unlike British expeditions that seek to explore unknown places, this is a practice that relates the people to their landscape as home (Henderson & Vikander, 2007).

Czech outdoor education, sometimes called *Turistika*, also has a long tradition of journeying at home on foot, bike, ski, snow shoe and canoe. The country has one of the most extensive systems of way-marked trails in the world. In the last fifty years, while under Russian occupation, the Czech people sustained their culture by adapting turistika. Thousands of them left the cities in the summer to live in camps in the valleys, woods, and mountains. Here, away from the eyes of the occupying people, they celebrated their culture through sport, outdoor activities, music, and food. In this case, journeying was a used as a way to maintain the culture of a people rather than explore the cultures of other people (Neuman, 2000).

Whether it is the trails and wilderness journeys of Americans, the voyageurs of Canada or the tramping of Kiwis, each culture has its way of travelling and of adapting this to educational ends that are rooted in its own history. Each form has its own practices and meanings unique to that country. Each can teach us something that may shed light on our own practices or offer our practices new possibilities.

CONCLUSIONS

This chapter has explored the historical and cultural origins of some of the values and practices that underpin British youth expeditions. Many of these are reproduced, in the UK and elsewhere, with each generation of explorers and youth expeditions. Each time, they may be reinterpreted for the times or they may be adopted without thought as simply "good practice". Although many expeditions may demonstrate good practice and meaningful educational experiences, it is important to critically appraise the underlying values of your plans before adopting, adapting, or rejecting them as part of your programme. The chapter that considers expedition ethics will help you more with this task.

Whenever a set of practices is adopted from one context into another, from the world of expeditions to the world of youth expeditions or from one culture into another for example, it creates an opportunity to reproduce or transform these practices. Youth expeditions will continue to review their approaches as they respond to the changing world around them. New global perspectives on environmental, social, political, and economic issues will continue to provide both challenges and opportunities for youth expeditions. Perhaps it is this engagement with the issues faced by the world that can provide the strongest rationale for British style youth expeditions in the face of rising ethical pressures associated with the social and environmental consequences of travel.

IMPLICATIONS FOR PRACTICE

– *Consider the degree to which your expedition's plans are "imperialistic".* Much expeditioning has involved explorers seeing the world through the eyes of what is/has been considered to be a superior culture. Review your plans to ensure elements of imperialistic tendencies do not seep in unintentionally. We all see "others" through our own eyes, with the filters of our own cultural heritage. Ask yourself questions about how you view your relationship with the place and the people you are visiting.

– *Consider the extent to which your plans based on "macho" concepts of conquest.* Part of the expedition tradition has been the high value placed on conquering people and, especially, places. It is unlikely that today's youth expeditions retain such attitudes to the people of another country. However, the conquest of summits and other such physical goals might be worth a pause for thought. While achievements such as these can be of great value, some have linked aspects of these approaches to certain masculine values or "macho" behaviour that may still prevail even in mixed sex expeditions.

– *Ask the question, "Who benefits from the expedition?".* While some mountaineers celebrate their achievements in egocentric ways, most hold a profound respect for nature and exercise considerable humility in talking about their exploits. However, even this, if not tempered with other elements in the programme, encourages an attitude to nature that is entirely instrumental. This happens when programmes are planned in which the participants benefit in many kinds of ways from the place (and the people) without returning the favour. We sometimes pay too little attention to the benefits we can leave behind. For example, understanding ourselves as having something to give a local people can be patronising if the local people do not feel as if they have something to give in return.

– *How does your expedition deal with the challenges of exclusivity?* Historically, most explorers have been predominantly white, wealthy males. While this has changed drastically in the last fifty years, one of the main contrasts between a uk expedition and journeys in scandinavia or the czech republic is their continued potential for exclusivity. This can be on many grounds. Only recently has female participation equalled that of males. Many youth expedition organisations are working hard on other dimensions, such as disability, social and educational background, and financial means. Obviously, all of these factors are increased for expeditions that go abroad to costly and remote places.

– *Weigh the benefits of a package versus a diy approach.* Throughout youth expedition history there has been a conundrum between the value for a local group of organising their own journey with their adult leaders and community

IMPLICATIONS FOR PRACTICE *(Continued)*

---

in support, versus the benefits of combining forces with specialists on a regional or national scale. The first has many obvious educational benefits, while the latter can often foster more ambitious plans – usually at the expense of the young people having less involvement in planning and preparation.

DISCUSSION QUESTIONS

1. Pretend that you are organising a trip to climb Mount Kilimanjaro with a group of university students. Considering Africa's colonial past, what are some of the issues that need attention during the planning process?

2. You have the opportunity to travel with a school group to remote villages living a largely subsistence life style, with limited education and health care, and occasional signs of malnutrition. Consider the relative merits of trading for your food and accommodation with local currency; books, medicines or vitamin rich foods; an exchange of songs and dances. Or should you take your own food and shelter?

3. Imagine that, as part of the education of young environmental scientists, you are considering a month-long trip to a remote and fragile ecosystem where the ability to self-rescue a casualty is essential. As vehicles are not an option, this will require a large group of people for safety reasons. Weigh the benefits of making the visit in order to document the wildlife and landforms against the impact of a large group on the wildlife, vegetation, and soils. What are the arguments on each side for making the trip or choosing another destination?

REFERENCES

Allcock, D. (2002). *Development training: A personal view*. Unpublished manuscript.
Bate, J. (2000). *The song of the earth*. London: Picador.
Black, J. (2003). *The British abroad: The Grand Tour in the eighteenth century*. Stroud, UK: The History Press.
British Schools Exploring Society. (2009). *Our history*. Retrieved August 31, 2009, from http://www.bses.org.uk/content/our-history/
Brookes, A. (2002). Gilbert White never came this far south. Naturalist knowledge and the limits of universalist environmental education. *Canadian Journal of Environmental Education, 7*(2), 73–87.
Chapman, R. (1986). *In the eye of the wind: The story of Operation Drake, the starting of Operation Raleigh*. London: Lorrimer.
Coleridge, S. T. (2008). *The rime of the ancient mariner*. London: Arcturus Foulsham.
Cranfield, I. (Ed.). (2002). *Inspiring achievement*. Penrith, UK: Institute for Outdoor Learning.
Desmond, R. (2007). *The history of Kew*. London: Royal Botanic Gardens.
Dybeck, M. (1996). *A broad river*. Ambleside, UK: Brathay Hall Trust.
Ellis, R., & Ellis, R. (2001). *Vertical margins: Mountaineering and the landscapes of neo-imperialism*. Madison, WI: University of Wisconsin Press.
Escritt, A. (1985). *Iceland: Handbook for expeditions*. London: Iceland Information Centre.

Fleming, F. (2001). *Killing dragons: The conquest of the Alps*. London: Granta Books.

Glyptis, S. (1991). *Countryside recreation*. Oxford, UK: Longman.

Grey, E. (1984). Expedition ethics. *Journal of Adventure Education and Outdoor Leadership, 3*(1), 25–26.

Hanbury-Tenison, R. (1993). *The Oxford book of exploration*. Oxford, UK: Oxford University Press.

Henderson, B. (2008). Experientially teaching Canadian travel: Literature on the trail and in the classroom. In L. Christensen, M. Long, & F. Waage (Eds.), *Teaching North American environmental literature* (pp. 392–402). New York: The Modern Language Association.

Henderson, B., & Vikander, N. (Eds.). (2007). *Nature first: Outdoor life the Friluftsliv way*. Toronto, Canada: Natural Heritage Books.

Kennedy, A. (1992). *The expedition experience as a vehicle for change in the inner city*. Penrith, UK: Adventure Education.

McCulloch, K. H. (2004). Ideologies of adventure: Authority and decision making in sail training. *Journal of Adventure Education and Outdoor Learning, 4*(2), 185–198.

Neuman, J. (2000). *Turistika sporty v prirode*. Prague: Portal.

Price, U. (2000). *On the picturesque*. Yeadon, UK: Woodstock Press.

Smith, M. (1997a). *Kurt Hahn*. Retrieved August 9, 2004, from http://www.infed.org/thinkers/et-hahn.htm

Smith, M. (1997b). *Robert Baden-Powell as an educational innovator*. Retrieved August 8, 2002, from www.infed.org/thinkers/et-bp.htm

Smith, M. (2002). *Ernest Thompson Seton and Woodcraft*. Retrieved July 15, 2002, from http://www.infed.org/thinkers/seton.htm

Taylor, J. (2008). *The voyage of the Beagle: Darwin's extraordinary adventure in Fitzroy's famous survey ship*. London: Conway.

Young Explorers Trust. (2009). *The young explorers trust*. Retrieved August 26, 2009, from http://www.theyet.org.uk

Chris Loynes
University of Cumbria/Threshold

PAUL STONEHOUSE

2. VIRTUE ETHICS AND EXPEDITIONS

"It'll develop your character"

This phrase is often used in reference to tasks that are both arduous and challenging. Perhaps this is why there has been a long-term association between character formation and expeditions. Yet what exactly is meant by the term "character"? It seems like a broad word used more anecdotally than in any kind of precise way. This confusion surrounding the concept of character makes claiming its relevance to any kind of education less trustworthy. It may therefore be helpful to critically examine the notion of character with the aim of clarifying its meaning and its specific pertinence to expeditionary education. This chapter provides one way – an ancient and philosophical way – of conceiving character.

Aristotle's virtue ethics are often referred to as character ethics, since the concept of character runs continuously throughout his ethical system. While virtue ethics is just one possible lens through which moral development on an expedition can be viewed, I have found it helpful in elucidating seemingly contrary research findings, as well as making sense of my own experiences, both as a participant and as an instructor.

The following pages provide an overview of Aristotle's understanding of character, and highlight why it is so relevant to expeditions.

VIRTUE ETHICS, CHARACTER, AND EXPEDITIONS

The principal text in which Aristotle (384–322 BCE) described his virtue ethics is the *Nicomachean Ethics* (Trans., 1999), which was most likely named after his son, Nicomachus. Being of such renown and influence in western philosophical education, the text is referred to by many as simply, *The Ethics*.

It is interesting to note that the purpose of *The Ethics* was not to provide a cogent, watertight moral argument about character, but to provide an understanding of how we, as humans, can become good (II 1§1)[1]. Aristotle immediately recognised the complexity of his endeavour. The good? Who can say for sure what that might be? He then acknowledged that the exacting theories and facts yielded within other disciplines, could never be expected from the field of ethics. When inquiring into moral matters, we are speaking in generalities at best (I 3§1–4).

Although abstract, Aristotle's acknowledgement of the limits of knowing within the ethical sphere is very pertinent to our current expeditionary discussion. He, in a sense, warns us, as researchers and practitioners, not to expect more certainty than is warranted by the subject of ethics. As researchers, we should be suspect of

S. K. Beames (ed.), Understanding Educational Expeditions, 17–23.
© *2010 Sense Publishers. All rights reserved.*

any attempt to use quantifying methods to measure ethical change – the subject simply doesn't warrant this kind of precision. It follows that, as practitioners, despite a financial donor's wish for "numbers-based research", we must find other viable ways to justify the moral worth of our programmes.

Aristotle, continuing with his investigation of the good, asked what it was that humankind strove for? After considering a variety of options, he decided on *eudaimonia* – translated as happiness, a flourishing life, fulfillment, or well-being – as our chief end (I 7§8). Aristotle believed that all species had these ends to which they generally strove, and that reaching these ends was a matter of being in harmony with the central function towards which the species was oriented. Just as a "good" plant typically absorbs light and grows, and a "good" fish swims, and "good" bird flies, Aristotle wondered what it was that made a human "good"? He believed that reasoning was the unique function of the human species (I 7§13). For him, our capacity and potential to reason was what set us apart from other life forms. Thus, for Aristotle, in order for a human to have a flourishing life, he or she must live in accordance with right reason. However, he acknowledged that each end towards which each species strove, could be attained well or poorly. Aristotle believed the aim of each species was to try to achieve virtue (literally excellence) and avoid vice (virtue's opposite) with respect to one's end. Humans, therefore, should strive for excellence in their reasoning. He closed this part of his argument with one more condition: that this virtuous ability to reason must be sought over one's lifetime in order for *eudaimonia* to be experienced. For Aristotle, the sum of virtue and vice over a lifetime was a person's character (I 10§11). The rest of *The Ethics* expounds his understanding of virtuous right reason.

This rather tedious argument offers several relevant considerations for expeditions. Most notably, Aristotle's condition that character is formed over a lifetime places serious constraints on our expectations to see moral change in our participants over a two to four week period. For Aristotle, we can only really speak of character in the hindsight of a life lived. If this is so, then what moral change, if any, should we expect our expeditions to have on our participants? Another relevant concern for expeditions is Aristotle's understanding of character primarily as a matter of right thinking, not necessarily physical challenge. If, instead, it is the physical challenge of expeditions that we deem relevant to character formation, in what way, if any, are expeditions relevant to developing right reason? That is, if one takes Aristotle's perspective, do expeditions help develop right reason, and therefore character?

This tension between character revealed through reason and character revealed through physical means is resolved in Aristotle's understanding of virtue. For him, virtue is both intellectually and physically expressed. In books III 6 – IV, he discusses what are often called the "moral virtues". These virtues (e.g. courage and self-control) are only possible if the body is able to listen to and obey the mind's convictions. In book VI, he discusses the "intellectual virtues". It is the intellectual virtues that decide the course of action that the body must act upon. However, if the moral virtues are not developed, it is unlikely that the body will follow through with the intellectual virtues' decision. On an expedition, we might see our participants' ability to carry 60lb backpacks for ten off-trail miles over 5000 feet of elevation as expressions of their moral virtue of endurance. Similarly, their decision that this strenuous endeavor is in some way worth their perseverance (another moral virtue) could be seen as an expression of their intellectual virtues. But how do we arrive at these decisions?

Aristotle, in book III 1–4, sketched how we arrive at these virtuously moral decisions. He set up a logical chain of events: 1) first we must want for the right things; 2) then we must perceive our circumstances correctly; 3) then we deliberate towards the right decision, given the context we've perceived; 4) and we finally make a moral decision given the three previous steps. This entire process is under the auspice of *phronēsis*: the intellectual virtue responsible for thinking well with regard to one's practical decisions (VI 1§5). As Aristotle's logic chain suggests, right behavior is not enough. One must have intentionally thought through the decision to have acted virtuously. As practitioners then, our educational efforts should not merely be to acquire a wanted behaviour from our participants, but to facilitate and encourage their moral decision-making ability: their *phronēsis*. At a curricular level, we should aim to include activities that challenge both intellectual virtue through decision-making, and moral virtue through challenging physical endeavors. The modern reader, coming from a more pluralistic position, may now be getting uncomfortable with Aristotle's notion that there are "right things" that lead to virtue. Isn't one person's virtue another person's vice? Aristotle pointed to the "right things" in his definition of a virtue:

> Virtue, then, is a state that decides, consisting in a mean, the mean relative to us, which is defined by reference to reason, that is to say, to the reason by reference to which the prudent person would define it. It is a mean between two vices, one of excess and one of deficiency. (II 7§15)

As the above definition suggests, Aristotle did believe in right reason. As a guide to this right reason, he proposed looking to "prudent" people - people with the intellectual virtue of *phronēsis* (the virtue that allows one to come to good moral decisions). While Aristotle didn't see morality as relative, he didn't really speak in terms of right or wrong either. Something was simply more virtuous or less virtuous. He believed that we could look towards people who generally have a flourishing, fulfilled and happy life as guides to our moral decision-making. Since these people, using *phronēsis*, have cultivated lives that have brought them well-being, their lives serve as moral examples for the decisions we make. Despite the many different values that hold sway throughout our lives (e.g. money, power, success) and bring apparent happiness, there seems to be a remarkable unity in what our elders hold dear as they approach the end of their lives. These "death-bed" values - the distillation of what is important in life - are the virtues that bring about *eudaimonia* (our chief end, happiness). Aristotle would probably suggest that as expedition leaders, we are to model a life of character, guided by *phronēsis*, and in so doing, be the crucial examples that our participants need to develop their own moral decision-making, character, and *phronēsis*. However, although being a moral example is essential, it presumably isn't enough. We must also construct curricula that encourage this ethical development.

Aristotle indirectly suggests three different catalysts that help foster *phronēsis* and the other virtues: reflection, practice, and the shared life. Reflection is at the heart of experiential learning theory, the philosophy of education most often associated with expeditions. It is also at the heart of character development for Aristotle. As we experience life, reflection allows us to glean moral lessons from our experience, which in turn allows us to apply these lessons in appropriate contexts in our future experiences (see VI 8§8–9 and VI 11§3–5). Too often on our expeditions, time to reflect is squeezed out by the temptation to maximise adventurous activity. Aristotle's teachings remind us that moral growth cannot occur without significant space for group and individual reflection.

Practicing moral decisions and actions provides the data for our reflection. Through practice, and reflection on it, we refine our *phronēsis*. Gradually, through our practice, we build predispositions, or habits of acting in certain ways. Some of these habits are helpful (e.g. self-control), some are not (e.g. over-eating). For a good action to be considered virtuous, it can't just be an infrequent occurrence in one's life. A virtuously honest action is an action done by an honest person. An honest person has cultivated the virtue of honesty in his or her life through countless honest actions that eventually establish a habit of honesty. This was why Aristotle said, "We become just by doing just actions and become temperate by doing temperate actions" (II 4§1). That character depends on virtue, and virtue depends on habit, makes the prospect of developing one's character a slow business. This again cautions us to have realistic expectations on the moral change we hope for in our participants. Can firm habits be established in two to four week expeditions? Instead of focusing on radically changing our participants' character, Aristotle might see it as more educationally reasonable to provide students with an abundance of opportunities for moral practice.

Virtue is learned through community. As already mentioned, we need others that are practically wise to guide us in our development. We also benefit from our peers – what Aristotle called "partners in deliberation" (III 3§19) – who struggle towards morality with us. More fundamentally, we need others in order to practice our virtuous actions. However, Aristotle doesn't limit the moral influence of others to merely the living. Literature, story, and myth also play important roles in our moral development (see III 1§8, 17). Whether through the example of an instructor's character, the community relationships established through journeying together, or the intentional readings chosen, expeditions have tremendous potential, through their shared life, to effect ethical growth. Yet, is this anticipated growth really development of character?

Aristotle provides a helpful way to understand character development. As noted earlier, virtue's opposite is vice. These two concepts, virtue and vice, are the extremes on a continuum. In between these termini exists the territory for our character development (see Fig. 1).

A virtue is the mean between two extremes of vice: one of excess, one of deficiency. For example, the virtue of courage is a mean between a vice of excess (rashness) and a vice of deficiency (cowardice). Vice is flagrantly and intentionally giving oneself to the opposite of virtue. Moving in from these extremes, we encounter

VIRTUE

Continence	Continence
Incontinence	Incontinence
Vice of excess	Vice of deficiency

Figure 1. Aristotle's gradations from virtue to vice in both directions.

the word incontinence, less familiarly meaning a lack of self-restraint, or an inability to control the will. An incontinent person knows the virtuous mean, and wants to do the virtuous mean, but is tempted to do otherwise, and commits an action contrary to the mean (see VII 8§1). As with vice, this contrary action can be done in excess or deficiency. Continuing to approach the mean, the continent person, who does have restraint, is still very tempted to commit a contrary action (see VII 1§6). However, their will being strong enough, they resist the temptation of the contrary action, and perform the action dictated by the mean. So, if character is the sum of virtue and vice over a lifetime (I 10§11), and we are continually moving on the moral continuum from incontinence, to continence, to virtue, for each virtue in our life, then our character is in a constant state of flux, albeit gradual and slow. Following Aristotle's argument, then, our character is constantly developing. So, in what sense do expeditions play any distinctive role in character development that is not already occurring in our conventional lives?

When asked how an expedition was relevant to her character, a participant of mine answered:

> Outdoor education offers a new way of seeing, a new reality. It's up to me whether I take what I've learned from the expedition and what I've realised from it…and do something with it in the future…. You get your eyes opened to something and then you choose to practice that behavior, …but unless it is reinforced, it will never change your character.

"A new way of seeing….". I think this phrase best communicates an expedition's moral contribution to a person's learning. It is arguable that we learn from others and about ourselves in a much more concentrated way while journeying together through the wilds. We learn to see ourselves, others, and the land differently. The reflective space and communal life, coupled with the inspiration of the landscape, produce a moral laboratory that invites ethical examination.

Let us return to the question at hand. Do expeditions develop character? I would answer with a qualified "yes". At a micro-level, significant (and important!) ethical work is happening during an expedition. However, only time will tell whether these new realisations, convictions, and understandings will form into habitual virtues, and thus ultimately develop character. For some, this may be a deflating conclusion. I don't see it that way. To provide an experience, especially in such a short span of time, where a participant learns to see differently, is no small achievement! This conclusion reminds expedition leaders to facilitate end-of-the-journey debriefs that encourage participants to articulate how they see differently. And finally, no expedition stands alone. For a new way of seeing to become a new way of being, our participants will require continued support and care long after the expedition ends.

Perhaps it is now more apparent why research on the lasting effects of expeditions - moral or otherwise - can seem conflicted. Significantly, new ways of seeing are created on the expedition, and many participants can articulate them to researchers shortly thereafter. A percentage of these participants will integrate, implement, and maintain these new discoveries within their lives. Others will, for a variety of reasons, shrink back to the stronger habits that held sway before the expedition. These insights have certainly helped me to make sense of my own experiences, as well. On many occasions I've had what I thought were "life-changing" events, only to find myself unchanged by them as time went by. Yet, I can also recount a notable number of events that have taken root and generated lasting change. But it's not that simple. Who can say how the moral seeds planted on expeditions that have not yet germinated may affect future experiences? Surely this potential alone makes our efforts worthwhile.

IMPLICATIONS FOR PRACTICE

- Ethical inquiry yields only generalities. We must find ways other than quantified research to justify our programmes.

- If character is developed over a lifetime, character development within a month-long expedition doesn't seem very probable. It might be better to speak of building "character awareness."

- When planning expeditions, we should aim to include activities that challenge both intellectual virtue through decision making, as well as moral virtue through challenging physical endeavors.

- Aristotle would call leaders to be the moral examples of character that participants need to develop their own moral decision-making, character, and *phronēsis*.

- Moral growth requires significant amounts for reflection. We must ensure that our expeditions do not become so overrun with adventurous activities that time for reflection is displaced.

- We become virtuous by doing virtuous actions. Our expeditionary curriculum must provide ample opportunity for moral practice.

- It is the social dynamic of expeditions that provides the fodder for ethical decisions. Our curriculum should emphasize community activity. As expedition leaders, we should facilitate end-of-the-journey debriefs, which encourage participants to articulate how they see differently.

DISCUSSION QUESTIONS

1. Given Aristotle's explanation of character development, what do you think is a reasonable expectation for moral growth on your expedition?

2. In what ways would you like to have your participants see differently?

3. How could your expedition facilitate growth in both the intellectual virtue of *phronēsis* (moral decision-making), and the more physically-based virtues (e.g. endurance)?

4. In what way can you ensure and protect reflective space on your expedition?

5. How can you create more opportunities for moral practice on your expedition?

6. In what ways can you promote social (and by default *moral*) interaction on your expedition?

7. What might be an appropriate end of the expedition debrief that facilitates the participants in articulating what they've ethically learned?

NOTES

[1] When citing Aristotle's Nicomachean Ethics (e.g. VI 5§2), the following notation is used. The Roman numeral is the book number (of which there are ten) within the Nicomachean Ethics (Book "VI" in the above example), the number after the Roman numeral (5) is the chapter within the book. The number after the "§" symbol is the section within the chapter.

REFERENCES

Aristotle. (1999). *Nicomachean ethics* (T. Irwin, Trans., 2nd ed.). Indianapolis, IN: Hackett.

Brookes, A. (2003). A critique of neo-Hahnian outdoor education theory. Part one: Challenges to the concept of "character building". *Journal of Adventure Education and Outdoor Learning, 3*(1), 49–62.

Brookes, A. (2003). A critique of neo-Hahnian outdoor education theory. Part two: The "fundamental attribution error" in contemporary outdoor education discourse. *Journal of Adventure Education and Outdoor Learning, 3*(2), 119–132.

FURTHER READING

Aristotle. (2000). *Nicomachean ethics* (R. Crisp, Trans.). Cambridge: Cambridge University Press.

Hunt, J., & Wurdinger, S. (1999). Ethics and adventure programming. In J. C. Miles & S. Priest (Eds.), *Adventure programming* (pp. 123–131). State College, PA: Venture.

Hursthouse, R. (2001). *On virtue ethics*. New York: Oxford University Press.

Milch, R., & Patterson, C. (1966). *Aristotle's Nicomachean ethics: Notes, including Aristotle's life, Aristotle's works*. Lincoln, NB: Cliffs Notes.

Wurdinger, S. (1987). The ethics of teaching virtue. *Journal of Experiential Education, 10*(1), 31–33.

Paul Stonehouse
Simpson University

SIMON BEAMES

3. INTERACTIONISM AND EXPEDITIONS

I have always intuitively thought that social situations characterised by unfamiliar people, places, and activities had the capacity to offer rich opportunities for all kinds of learning and growth. Still, how can one explain this on a theoretical level? Although there are, arguably, a number of possible explanations, one conceptual framework that I find particularly useful is *interactionist* social theory.

Sociologists are interested in how individuals shape, and are shaped by, society. Indeed, since the study of society was formalised in the late 1800s, this tension between the ways in which society influences people, and is in turn influenced by people, has been ever-present (Layder, 1994).

Many sociologists see this tension on a spectrum of social theory, with larger structural forces at one end (e.g. governments, economics) and individual's actions (aka "agency") at the other. Many social theories have tried to resolve this structure/agency dualism, but none has been widely accepted as being entirely successful.

As an alternative to finding the "best" sociological theory, it may make more sense to use the theory most suited to the circumstances being studied. In the case of expeditions, I find *interactionist* social theory especially helpful in explaining the ways in which humans are influenced by the people, places, and ideas that they encounter during expeditions.

In this chapter, I will offer a very brief history of interactionism and outline key ideas from seminal thinkers such as Mead, Cooley, Blumer, and Goffman. Throughout the chapter, and especially at the end, I will offer examples of how interactionist theory provides us with ways of more deeply understanding expedition life.

HISTORY

The home of interactionism is the University of Chicago, which was also home to the pragmatist movement of the early 20th century. Although John Dewey is the best known of the pragmatists – particularly to outdoor experiential educators – it was his colleague George Herbert Mead (1863–1931) who laid the foundation for interactionism.

It is interesting to note that although Mead used the phrase "symbolic interactionism", he did not label his thoughts with this moniker. He was known to most as a social psychologist. It was Blumer, Mead's former student, who

S. K. Beames (ed.), Understanding Educational Expeditions, 25–32.
© *2010 Sense Publishers. All rights reserved.*

popularised the term "symbolic interactionism" through the publication of his book of the same name in 1969. Another interesting note is that Mead's book *Mind, self, and society* was published in 1934 - three years after his death. If the book does not read as being particularly cohesive, this is partly due to it being more of a collection of his, and his students', lecture notes.[1] Blumer continued Mead's work at the University of Chicago for the next 27 years.

The next player I want to introduce is Charles Horton Cooley (1864–1929). Cooley was a sociologist at the University of Michigan, and a contemporary of Mead's. Although Cooley published widely on a range of topics, he remains especially known for one concept that is of fundamental importance for interactionists: the looking glass self. More on this below!

The final author to be considered is Erving Goffman (1922–1982). Goffman completed his MA and PhD at the University of Chicago. Although he did not study under Blumer, his ideas clearly draw from work by Mead and Cooley. His conceptual framework of dramaturgy, outlined in his 1959 book *The presentation of self in every day life*, is probably the most widely-read interactionist work.

KEY IDEAS

Blumer

Humans are constantly acting towards physical, social, and abstract objects, according to Blumer (1969). Physical objects are inanimate, such as chairs, cars, and trees. Social objects are people, and abstract objects refer to intangible concepts such as justice and courage.

Armed with the assumption of humans acting towards objects, Blumer outlined three premises of symbolic interactionism. The first is that individuals act towards objects based on the meanings they have for them. The second premise is that meanings arise out of interaction with those objects. Blumer's third premise is that meanings are constantly being interpreted and modified by people's interaction with objects. So, meanings are not fixed. There may be other meanings that a person can attach to a given object that they may not know, as they have not yet interacted with that object in a certain way. Now, much of this may seem glaringly obvious, but it does serve to offer a clear (yet basic) theoretical explanation of how humans come to "think" and "do".

Blumer's premises help us understand how, on an expedition, the meanings that the young people attach to social, physical and abstract objects are not fixed, but are constantly being adjusted as a consequence of their interactions with these objects. Blumer (1969) describes this as a process where "objects are being created, affirmed, transformed, and cast aside" (p. 12). As an individual interacts with objects they have an internal conversation, interpreting and transforming meaning "in light of the situation" (Blumer, 1969, p. 5). So, novel interpretations can be offered by expeditions that bring people into contact with either unfamiliar objects or different ways of acting towards familiar objects. These kinds of interactions have the capacity to influence people's attitudes and behaviours.

Mead

A large part of interactionism's usefulness in understanding how people experience expeditions lies in what Mead (1934) refers to as the genesis of the self. A critical part of a child's development involves becoming able to take on the role of the "other" and visualise oneself from the other's point of view. This suggests that people's thoughts and behaviours are influenced by those around them; an individual's reflexivity with his or her social world is a constant and dynamic relationship that shapes who they are.

Mead (1934) argued that the final stage of human maturation involved taking the role of *the generalised other* – the attitude of the whole community. Rather than individuals merely considering their own needs and feelings, they also consider others' attitudes "towards various phases or aspects of the common social activity" (p. 155). The point crucial to Mead's thesis is that people's identities are formed by a combination of these collective attitudes and their own spontaneous, "unchecked" responses to their social circumstances. So, the generalised other "reflects the laws and the mores, the organized codes and expectations of the community" (p. 197) and serves to moderate immediate, unconsidered individual responses to the social situations in which people find themselves.

Whether in a classroom or on an expedition, interactionists believe that an individual's behaviour is heavily influenced by the company they keep. From Mead's perspective, going on an expedition with a familiar group of people might (in some ways) limit each individual's potential for personal growth, as the group members' collective expectations of each other will be no different that they were before the expedition began. Although the (presumably) novel physical environment of an expedition may influence the collective attitudes of the expedition community, Mead's argument suggests that if an expedition's goal is to elicit novel ways of "being" for individual participants, then it may be much easier to do this in circumstances where individuals have minimal knowledge of, and expectations of, each other.

Cooley

The notion of individuals considering other's attitudes and actions before acting was also conceptualised by Cooley (1927; 1962; 1964). Cooley's contribution to understanding the self centred on what he termed the *looking glass self*. Like Mead, Cooley (1927) believed that the self was formed by an individual's reflexive relationships with their social world, and regarded society as an "interweaving and interworking of mental selves. I imagine your mind, and especially what your mind thinks about my mind" (pp. 200–201). This belief formed the basis for the looking glass self, which is a three step process comprising "the imagination of our appearance to the other person, the imagination of his [sic] judgment of that appearance, and some sort of self-feeling" (Cooley, 1964, p. 184). The looking glass self contributes to this discussion by emphasising the critical importance of individuals interpreting others' interpretations. During interactions, individuals use their interpretative abilities to consider the outcomes of different courses of action before they act, as if through the eyes of others. Again, when considering the social make-up of expedition groups, individuals who have little idea of how others may respond to their thoughts or actions, may be less willing to do or say something that may be stigmatising, or outside of what the generalised attitudes of the group may consider "normal".

Another concept that informs Blumer's overall symbolic interactionist perspective is Cooley's (1962) primary group. This concept has particular relevance to expedition teams. In essence, Cooley referred to an individual's family and closer circle of friends as their primary group. The difference between a primary group and other people in society is that in a primary group people do not expect a personal benefit or gain from their relationships with other members of the group. This lies in contrast to non-primary group relationships, which tend to be characterised by an "exchange of specific services or benefits" (Coser, 1971, p. 308). People in primary groups will often do favours for each other without looking for specific compensation. For example, it is not unusual for expedition members to make hot drinks for each other or take turns washing up after a meal. Cooley (1962) described primary groups as being characterised by "intimate face to face association and cooperation. They are primary in several senses but chiefly in that they are fundamental in forming the social nature and ideals of the individuals" (p. 23).

The interaction between an individual and others on an expedition is most typically confined to relations within one's expedition team, which typically comprises 10 to 12 participants and two leaders. The members of this primary group have a different relationship between themselves and people outside this group, as their relationships are characterised by not expecting compensation for services rendered to each other, and an understanding that the good of the group has greater importance than the needs of one member (Cooley, 1962).

I am confident in assuming that most of us have experienced how, on an expedition, the group almost instantly becomes a primary group for its members; norms of giving, taking, sharing between people abound. Expeditions may be particularly powerful and unusual for some participants, as day-to-day living often necessitates strong norms of reciprocity between people who have only recently met. If participants are well-known to each other, this inter-reliance may occur at a deeper level on expedition than in more typical urban social circumstances.

Goffman

Another writer whose ideas inform the examination of social interaction on expeditions is Goffman (1959) and his dramaturgical conception of the self. As with other interactionists, Goffman sees the self as a product of social interactions, which, by employing language of the stage, he regarded as performances between actors and audiences.

The constructivist nature of Goffman's (1959) work shows how, at the beginning of an expedition, people may reveal different information about themselves. This information will vary, depending on, for example, if their audience is composed of prospective employers, a platoon of commandos, or their peers. The self projected by the actor will be directly influenced by the audience, who will also "project a definition of the situation by virtue of their response to the individual..." (p. 9). These selves are each deliberately crafted (though possibly subconsciously) in order to satisfactorily match the expectations that each audience has for the actor. We are actors and audience simultaneously.

A considerable part of impression management involves the actor using "expressive equipment" that is "intentionally or unwittingly employed" (Goffman, 1959, p. 32). This equipment enables the actor to present the audience with a front, which can be divided into one's appearance (e.g. clothing) and manner (e.g. gestures and speech patterns). An "idealised" front is derived from congruence between the actor's front and the expectations of the audience. The actor's identity is confirmed and strengthened by playing the same part to the same audience on different occasions. This explains how our identities within primary groups may be relatively fixed (e.g. in families). So, according to Goffman, depending on how well the individuals on an expedition know each other, a person's identity will be strongly influenced by what he/she perceives the expectations of the audience to be.

In Goffman's (1959) eyes, the audience become willing collaborators to the actor's performance, as they are asked "to believe that the character they see actually possesses the attributes he [sic] appears to possess" (p. 17). Seen this way, "communicative acts [are]... translated into moral ones" (p. 242). Goffman explains that implicit in an actor's performance is the request that the observers "take seriously the impression that is fostered before them" (p. 28), as he has exerted a "moral demand on the others" (p. 24) to treat him as if he possesses all of the characteristics that he would lead the audience to believe. In most cases, the audience will happily accept the performance presented to them, particularly if the performer is unfamiliar to the audience. Naturally, this will not be the case if the actor has a history of deceiving his audiences!

A vital aspect of Goffman's framework is the way in which individuals use "defensive and protective practices" in order to "safeguard the impression fostered by an individual during his [sic] presence before others" (p. 25). Indeed, Goffman's has considerable sociological interest based on his belief that "impressions fostered in every-day performances are subject to disruption" (p. 72). The intrigue lies in the ways in which people counter and minimise these disruptions to the impressions they are projecting. So, at the beginning of a two week river course, if an individual presents the front of a seasoned canoe-tripper, she will have to work hard at sustaining this impression for the rest of her time with this particular audience.

Goffman does not regard individuals as having one authentic self. Neither does he believe that people possess a number of masks that may be negotiated in order to reveal a core self. Rather, he sees humans as having multiple, fluid selves that are shaped by each social group interacted with. One self (or role) is not necessarily any more real or genuine than another.

CONCLUSIONS

Although the general ideas located within interactionist theory may offer convincing ways of understanding how people are influenced by their expedition group, there is also a (perhaps) disheartening corollary. If, while on expedition, individuals are so influenced by the looking glass self (Cooley, 1964), their primary groups (Cooley, 1962), the generalised other (Mead, 1934), and their various audiences (Goffman, 1959), there is no reason to suppose that they will be not be similarly influenced by the social circumstances they encounter post-expedition. For example, if a male young offender goes on an expedition with several non-offenders who happen to be very caring towards each other, he may display similar behaviour while in their company. However, there is every likelihood that when he returns to his original social pattern hallmarked by peers who steal cars, alcoholic parents, and relative poverty, he will revert to conducting himself in a way that matches the expectations of that social circle.

Herein lies a limitation of any "one off" outdoor education programme used for purposes of personal and social development. Although, as Blumer (1969) argues, being exposed to new ways of considering certain physical, social, and abstract objects may change a person's meanings for these objects, these meanings are not fixed and can easily revert to their pre-expedition constructions. This is a concept of critical importance, as it outlines how the generalised other "represents the forces of conformity and social control" (Ritzer, 1988, p. 299). The strength of this influence depends on the unity and interpersonal connections of the groups that are interacted with (Rock, 1979).

According to interactionist theory, people's identities are "never formed for once and for all time; they change as relationships change, and as we meet new people and face new situations" (Coakley & Pike, 2009, p. 52). So, in effect, everyone - before, during, and after an expedition - is constantly constructing meaning and shaping social life through interaction with other people and the conditions in which they find themselves. Interactionist theory may help expedition organisers, leaders, and associated agencies better understand the ways in which participants give meaning to their social world and how this meaning then guides their decisions and actions.

IMPLICATIONS FOR PRACTICE

– Interactionism explains how the meanings that people hold for physical, social, and abstract objects will be shaped by the places, people, and ideas with which they interact.

– The looking glass self, the primary group, the generalised other, and the presentation of self are concepts that explain how a participant's identity is heavily influenced by the social relations and interactions negotiated during the expedition.

– Just as these concepts outline the influences on how a person thinks and acts during an expedition, these same concepts explain how some of the personal and social development that may take place on an expedition can effectively become "undone" when participants return to the influence of their original social patterns.

DISCUSSION QUESTIONS

1. Describe an instance where you have seen the generalised/collective attitudes of a group influence individual behaviour.

2. If expedition participants revert to their pre-expedition attitudes and behaviours once they rejoin old social patterns, how can expedition organisers hope to combat these social constraints and effectively make expedition learning "endure"?

3. How might going on an expedition with participants from similar backgrounds, with similar aspirations, actually limit opportunities for personal growth?

NOTES

[1] Even today there are a number of unpublished articles of Mead's writing in existence. Many of these are housed online at http://www.brocku.ca/MeadProject/

REFERENCES

Blumer, H. (1969). *Symbolic interactionism: Perspective and method.* Berkeley, CA: University of California Press.
Coakley, J., & Pike, E. (2009). *Sports in society: Issues and controversies.* Maidenhead, UK: McGraw-Hill.

Cooley, C. H. (1927). *Life and the student*. New York: Alfred Knopf.

Cooley, C. H. (1962). *Social organization*. New York: Schocken.

Cooley, C. H. (1964). *Human nature and the social order*. New York: Schocken.

Coser, L. A. (1971). *Masters of sociological thought*. New York: Harcourt Brace Jovanovich.

Goffman, E. (1959). *The presentation of self in everyday life*. New York: Anchor.

Layder, D. (1994). *Understanding social theory*. London: Sage.

Mead, G. H. (1934). *Mind, self, and society: From the standpoint of a social behaviorist*. London: University of Chicago Press.

Ritzer, G. (1988). *Sociological theory*. New York: Alfred A. Knopf.

Rock, P. (1979). *The making of symbolic interactionism*. London: The MacMillan Press.

Simon Beames
The University of Edinburgh

BRENT BELL, SIMON BEAMES, AND WILL CARLSON

4. THE EXPEDITION AND RITES OF PASSAGE

The aims of this chapter are to provide an overview of the anthropological model of the rites of passage (ROP) and to discuss its usefulness for those leading educational expeditions. In our experience, it is not uncommon for outdoor educators to express the desire to use expeditions as rites of passage for young participants, most likely because of the similar structural components between ROPs and expeditions (Bell, 2003). Our aim is to outline potential applications of a rites of passage model on expeditions, while also highlighting pitfalls that may be associated with using the ROPs.

A rite of passage is a model of social transition with a common format observed across cultures. It was first conceived by the Belgian anthropologist, Arnold van Gennep in 1909 (van Gennep, 1960 [1909]). According to van Gennep, life is a series of passages from one stage to another. The rites of passage is composed of three rites: 1) *separation* from one's original social pattern, 2) *liminality,* a state of transition, and 3) *reincorporation* back into an existing social structure with a new role and/or status. The second rite, liminality, was extensively examined by the British anthropologist Victor Turner (1969), who claimed that this stage involved intense learning opportunities characterized by experiencing *communitas*: a coming together of people. Although rites of passage may focus on birth, childhood, marriage, or funerals, our primary interest is the transition from youth to adult. Figure 1 (below) provides an example of how rites of passage function. The figure highlights the movement of the initiate, beginning on the left and moving through the process of transition.

The topic of rites of passage has generated controversy among educators who believe that modern Western society lacks challenging and structured initiation rituals through which young people can mark their coming of age (Kornfield, 1996; Meade, 1996; Oldfield, 1996; Somé, 1996). Kornfield (1996) states that "if nothing is offered in the way of initiation to prove one's entry into the world of men and women, it will be done unguided in the road or the street with cars at high speed, with drugs, with weapons" (p. 42). Although rites of initiation exist in college fraternities and sororities, street gangs, and sports teams, these may not be entirely positive learning experiences (Meade, 1996; Somé, 1996). Despite the beneficial function of marking important transitions, rites of passage generally reinforce and support the status quo, which has led critics to voice concerns over indoctrination and the limiting influence the rites can have on participants' freedom of choice. An example of this is young women who are transitioning to roles of servitude in patriarchal societies (Prazak, 2007).

S. K. Beames (ed.), Understanding Educational Expeditions, 33–44.
© *2010 Sense Publishers. All rights reserved.*

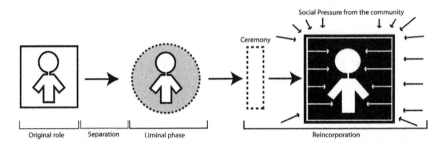

Figure 1. Model of the Rites of Passage.

Could the rites of passage have value for outdoor participants if guided by responsible and thoughtful educators? This paper is an exploration of how expeditions might be appropriate rites of passage for our society's young people.

In the child to adult transition, the participant leaves behind the role of child through a separation rite, which in some cases may include sudden physical separation of the child from the family (Kenhoe, 1998). Next, the participant enters a stage of liminality, which exists "betwixt and between" the child and adult social roles (Turner, 1969). During this period of socialization, participants will lack social referents that provided meaning in their former role (Ashford, 2001), which for outdoor educators can be likened to a state of adaptive dissonance (Walsh & Gollins, 1976). This shared dissonance (a.k.a. disequilibrium) can result in strong inter-personal bonds or communitas being formed (Ashford, 2001). This collective group feeling benefits the group through social support and teamwork, and by developing long-term ties between members.

In traditional societies, one factor that enhances the power of ROPs is guidance by community elders. Elders teach initiates the oral traditions of their people, often with particular attention paid to past struggles (Houston, 1996; Van Wyk, 2002). Another traditional factor is the use of solitude as a means to encourage youth to reflect on who they are and how they intend to take on the role of an adult within their community (Gibbons, 1974; Maddern, 1990; Suler, 1990).

The primary vehicle for socialization, however, is through facilitation of a challenging experience, such as a journey, that is rich with metaphorical meaning. For example, climbing a mountain, surviving time alone, and hunting animals are each metaphorically connected with the challenges of the adult role. Completing such challenges is one way that initiates may demonstrate their fitness for adulthood (Ashford, 2001).

The third and last stage of rites of passage is reincorporation. Typically, this stage is marked with a celebration that recognizes the end of liminality and grants new social status to the initiates. Figure 1 (earlier in the chapter) distinguishes reincorporation with arrows demonstrating the pressure that comes from the newly adopted role (inside the box) and with arrows (outside the box) that denote social pressure from the community.

We now highlight different aspects common to rites of passage and discuss their similarities to expeditions.

RITES OF PASSAGE AND EXPEDITIONS: ASSESSING THE SIMILARITIES

Separation

The stage of separation in the rites of passage and leaving on an expedition both function in the same way. Both remove the participants from their usual day-to-day life and impel them into what Keith King calls, "A new and vigorous learning environment" (personal communication, March 24, 2009). Although this removal may occasionally be quite sudden, it is often anticipated by the initiate.

Liminal Experience

Liminality is a social situation where participants exist between their former and future roles. Initiates look to the guides in order to understand the norms and expectations associated with the new situation because the initiates are expected to extinguish the behaviors of their prior role and take on the behaviors of their future role. For example, on an expedition, students learn new skills for managing self-care and personal safety. As teenagers back home they may have successfully met their needs through manipulation and bargaining in their social group. In the novel expedition environment, such skills may not be useful or applicable.

Elders/Guides

The use of guides during the liminal stage helps to direct personal change. Guides encourage behaviors that enable participants to more appropriately adapt to demands of the stage. Guides and elders facilitate the challenges in ways that a leader might on an expedition. In most cases, guides on rites of passage and on expeditions have lived through the experience of the initiates. In essence, they provide a set of circumstances for the initiate consistent with what they themselves have experienced. Usually, this involves challenging the initiates with an appropriate amount of physical and emotional obstacles, with the aim of eliciting a powerful educational experience.

Symbols and Ritual Objects

Guides will often introduce meaningful symbols to the group. For example, the group might be introduced to a flag, which is symbol of their culture. Symbols like this can become powerful reminders and mediators of community norms. Likewise, on an expedition, symbols like rope bracelets, t-shirts, pins, patches, and hats can offer normative reminders of group expectations.

Communitas and Group Bonding

Group bonding, feelings of closeness, and *communitas* as defined by Turner (1969), are common to rites of passage and expeditions. Instead of individual feelings separating the students from each other, "shared feelings" elicited from shared experiences often serve to bond the group together. This feeling of closeness and unity is familiar to outdoor leaders and is a factor in the successful use of rites of passage.

Purposeful Time and Space

Rites of passage are constrained by time and space. Participants know the rites will come to an end, so the rites offer a limited time for completion of challenges put before them. Participants enter a rite of passage with a goal in mind, which is similar to an expedition that sets out to climb a mountain or travel a specific route. Both experiences have temporal boundaries, which inevitably render returning home an aspect of the rite. The great outdoor educator, Willie Unsoeld, described purposeful time and space when he explained that Outward Bound's goal was to prepare people to go back to society with greater purpose rather than promote separation from society (Unsoeld, 1985).

Solitary Reflection

Spending time alone is another common feature of the liminal stage. Initiates' reflections on who they are and how they intend to assume a new role in the community during the liminal stage are enhanced by solo time (Gibbons, 1974; Maddern, 1990; Suler, 1990). The use of the solo on expedition has also demonstrated beneficial outcomes to participants and has since become an accepted component of many longer expeditions (Bobliya, McAvoy, & Kalisch, 2005).

Scripts

Another common theme between an expedition and the rites of passage is the scripting of the new role. A script can contain a new vocabulary, as well as appropriate rules for communication and conduct (Ashforth, 2001; Dalton-Puffer, 2007). During the liminal phase, the initiates are provided sets of scripts to use in their new role. Just as a student preparing to play a role in a theatrical production is given scripts, practice, and feedback from directors, participants in rites of passage are provided with words, symbols, and guidance on how to enact a new role. This is also apparent on expedition programs that "script" accepted ways to deal with such things as interpersonal conflict (e.g. using "I" statements and Full Value Contracts).

Reincorporation and Social Pressure

The last, and perhaps most difficult stage to facilitate, is the reincorporation stage. In this stage the initiate returns to the former social group, but in a new role. The reincorporation stage is important because it is here that social pressure from community members will reinforce newly established roles (Cushing, 1999). It is important to note that if some members of the community choose to promote roles that are inconsistent with those legitimized by the dominant social group, then competing social pressure may destroy or undo newly established roles. Reincorporation requires a large degree of community consensus regarding the role initiates will undertake within their community (Venable, 1997). The measure of success for a rite of passage can be thought of as the degree to which initiates perform their new roles within the social group.

These elements of rites of passage and those of an expedition appear to share many similar structures. Rites of passage are often important breaks from ordinary life that combine education, community, and celebration, but there are pitfalls associated with applying this theoretical framework to practice.

CRITIQUES AND PITFALLS

Critiques of using rituals for personal and social development focus primarily on their controlling and conforming nature. Rites of passage and rituals operate like social machinery influencing the norms, values, and structures of the social groups within a culture. Such machinery may serve to reproduce social structures that devalue individual differences (e.g. homosexuality) (Berry, 2006; Prazak, 2007). Rites of passage are also associated with practices such as hazing and genital mutilation. Female circumcision, for instance, "is practiced in societies where patriarchal authority and control over female sexuality and fertility are givens" (Althaus, 1997, p. 131). The rites of passage are meant to reinforce and uphold societal beliefs and once these rituals become traditions they are difficult to question and/or change. Because of these critics, rites of passage can also be seen as processes to avoid.

Others believe that humans have a deep-seated need for rites of passage, as modern life is largely devoid of meaningful ritual. Proponents of rites of passage see the lack of such rituals as detrimental to society.

We take the position that both sides have merit. Rites of passage are often associated with conformity and oppression; however, many people also desire ritual experiences that develop personal growth and social order. We encourage the use of thoughtful implementation of ritual in education with the proviso that it is carefully planned to avoid the traps and pitfalls that reproduce injustice. Since leaders on expeditions are expected to operate as guides and provide powerful educational experiences, a clear understanding of culturally appropriate ritual is important.

Misappropriation of Rites of Passage

A crucial point needs to be made regarding modern initiations based on traditional models. Although we discuss the creation of rites and rituals, we are not supporting the misappropriation of rites from other cultures. Educational models that involve non-indigenous people who adopt traditional rituals of indigenous people are difficult to justify. Horwood (1994) states that "misappropriation and trivialization of Native American ceremonies within...the practice of outdoor education, has drawn emphatic and articulate objections from both natives and non-natives" (p. 12). Native spiritual ceremonies have no part in the "educational, often recreational, secular purposes of non-natives" (p. 12). Therefore, non-indigenous people should seek out their own connections with the land and create ceremonies with greater relevance to participants' cultures.

Ignoring Reincorporation

Reincorporation is the most diffcult of the rites to create since it involves the active participation of a whole community - if not whole culture. Bell (2003) identified the contemporary adventure model (see Figure 2) based on the research of Cline (1993), Venable (1997) and Cushing (1998; 1999). The model demonstrates how numerous program participants on expeditions loosely based on the rites of passage models are left alone to manage their transition. This often places students in conflict with their old roles. Instead of the expedition helping to clarify personal understanding it may exacerbate confusion.

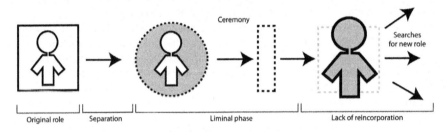

Figure 2. The contemporary adventure model (Bell, 2003): Rites of Passage without structured reincorporation.

CONCEPTUALIZING RITES OF PASSAGE

An important way to consider educational activities is to recognize the level of freedom and type of participation that allows students to influence the meaning and direction of the experience. At one end of the spectrum of leader influence is a constructivist space, where learners have total freedom to reflect upon experience without specific guidance. The other end of this spectrum is marked by highly defined norms that are imposed on the learners with ritualized activities, static knowledge and meanings, and prescribed scripts demanding adherence and conformity.

Our experience as educators is that students benefit from many approaches along a continuum - from constructivist educational experiences that focus on the learner directing the creation of knowledge to highly prescribed educational experiences employing ritual and metaphor. Regardless of the approach taken, course content and delivery methods associated with any educational programme need to be adequately justified.

A further structural issue is whether an expedition serves as a liminal space for a broader transition, or embedding the rites of passage within the expedition experience. These two distinctions are described in more detail below and highlighted in Figures 3 and 4.

Expedition as Liminal Phase

One example of an expedition as a liminal phase takes place in the form of an orientation programme for new students at an American college, as highlighted by Bell (2003). The participants in this example are transitioning from their previous role as high school students to their new role as college students. The liminal phase of the transition is a week-long backpacking trip that focuses on building social bonds, discussing community expectations, and preparing students to function within the college community.

The last challenge of the liminal experience is a 12 kilometer "marathon" from the last campsite to the college - a distance longer than most students have ever run. At the finish line, students are met by parents, faculty, and staff who celebrate their accomplishment and publicly recognize their new role as college students. In this transition, the outdoor orientation trip functions as the liminal phase. By recognizing the transition through the completion of a liminal experience the community is better able to support the participants in their new role as college students.

Rites of passage with expeditions as the liminal stage comprise four key elements. First, the guides communicate the college's ideals and values. Second, the group practices commitments to the group ideals, which results in being able to act out their new role more effectively. Third, initiates are provided with scripts and a new language, which allow them to operate more appropriately within the community. Finally, students develop a sense of communitas that will hopefully provide social support throughout their college experience.

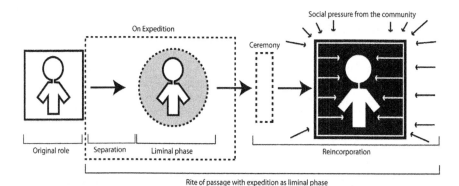

Figure 3. Rites of Passage using an expedition as the liminal stage.

ROP within a Program

The rites of passage contained within an expedition means that the role-shifts, reincorporations, and community support all come from within the expedition group (as opposed to a non-expedition social group). This is a common occurrence in some adventure therapy programmes. Upon entering a therapeutic program, students are removed from their home environment and brought to the wilderness as a form of initial separation. The student is then required to learn the rights and responsibilities espoused by that particular program. The student begins the therapeutic process in a low status role. During the expedition the student will one day be separated from this low status role and moved into a liminal phase, where they can enact certain behaviors that will prove their worth for the new status position. Once these skills are mastered, an appropriate ritual serves to redefine the rights and responsibilities of the individual within the group. This reincorporation into the group with a change in role often results in the student being more responsible for the decisions made within the group, as well as acting as a mentor to the other students.

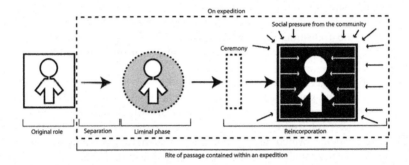

Figure 4. Rites of Passage Model with the transition contained within the expedition.

Incorporating Rites of Passage into an Expedition

Numerous expedition-based programmes have used rituals to enhance the educational impact of their trips. Below are some ideas connected to seven components of a rites of passage programme that may be familiar to outdoor leaders. Thinking about each component and how it can be enacted on an expedition is an important step in beginning to develop an informed ROP framework.

Rites of Separation: The ending of the original role (leaving home)

Creating a unique and vigorous liminal experience can enhance these rites. Typically, removing the participants from items that provide comfort in the past role is helpful (e.g. cell phones). The pack check is often a time of removing non-essential items, removing street clothes and jewelry – all of which help to define their former identity.

Rites of Liminality: Learning about the new role (training)

A lot of new information is provided at the beginning of an expedition. Examples include providing new language ("I" statements), role modeling, skills instruction, norm setting, and creating a Full Value Contract (FVC). These all reinforce the new expectations regarding participants' attitudes and behaviors.

Practice with the new role expectations (main expedition)

Examples include managing a trial period with leadership responsibilities, students managing conflict resolution, and upholding the FVC.

Symbolism to support the new role (items with special meaning)

Symbolism on trips varies widely. Leaders may create "talking sticks" that facilitate who talks and when and contracts written on ensolite pads. Other ways include carrying a program "legacy journal" with reports of successful transitions of others who came before. Some expedition groups will create their own unique symbols made on the trail or attempt to embed new meaning into group gear.

Practice with new role expectations (final expedition)

Students use their newly acquired knowledge in order to successfully and independently complete challenges set by the guides.

Rites of Reincorporation: Ritual to define the end of the transition (marathon)

A final challenge, such as a forest run of 10–40 kilometers can be a powerful metaphor with which to end the transition. Successful mastery of a physical challenge is meant to be representative of their ability to undertake future challenges, and thus demonstrate readiness for reincorporation.

Immediate identification of a successful passage (parents, staff, faculty, students' welcome at marathon finish)

Examples include adding to their story of success to the legacy journal, dividing the group flag, and graduation speeches that highlight commitments based upon the students' learning. Publicly, initiates may be honored at a ceremony, where they are provided with clothing or symbols to recognize their new status. Ideally, these visible symbols have power within the broader community, so these new meanings are recognized and reinforced.

An especially important aspect of developing effective rites of passage is defining roles for the initiates that are equally valued and desired by the initiates themselves and by the community. The broader the support of the rites, the better the chance of an effective role-transition. However, a rite of passage can take place within a smaller community, such as a wilderness expedition, a summer camp or college as we highlight above.

CONCLUSIONS

Many expedition programs largely mimic the ritual processes found in the rites of passage (Beames, 2004; Bell, 2003; Cushing, 1999; Venable, 1997). But when a rites of passage program is not supported and reinforced by others in the initiate's community, any personal transformation that took place is unlikely to endure. As much as expedition leaders may want to believe that they can foster lasting personal and social transformation, this outcome is probably far beyond their scope and ability.

Knowing how to manage liminal space, use ritual, and provide rites of passage to manage important role-transitions would appear to be critical facilitation skills that are within the realm of any mature, experienced, and thoughtful instructor. We believe that educators wishing to draw upon the rites of passage model for their course design should carefully consider appropriate ways that this can be accomplished. As Dewey (1938) points out, "there is no point in [a teacher]...being more mature if, instead of using his [sic] greater insight to help organize the conditions of the experience of the immature, he [sic] throws away his insight" (p. 38).

We support the employment of the rites of passage in educational contexts under the proviso that they involve the broader community and use culturally relevant rituals.

IMPLICATIONS FOR PRACTICE

- Involve a community in first defining, and then recognizing, the successful adoption of desirable social roles.

- Consider who is determining the rituals, symbols, and scripts. Do they come from the leaders or the participants?

- Ensure that ROP activities and rituals are not uncritically imported from another culture.

- Consider the intended meaning of the transition. Who benefits from the rites of passage and why?

DISCUSSION QUESTIONS

1. Using the seven identified attributes of the rites of passage, how could an expedition programme construct a curriculum for role transition?

2. If rites of passage promote conformity and undermine individual freedom, why are they attractive to social groups?

3. Why is reincorporation so important in the rites of passage model?

4. How could using the rites of passage model on an expedition backfire?

5. Imagine the best case scenario for a rite of passage on an expedition. What would occur in ideal circumstances?

REFERENCES

Althaus, F. (1997). Female circumcision: Rite of passage or violation of rights? *International Family Planning Perspectives, 23*(3), 130–133.

Ashforth, B. E. (2001). *Role transitions in organizational life: An identity-based perspective.* Mahwah, NJ: Lawrence Erlbaum Associates.

Beames, S. (2004). Overseas youth expeditions: A rite of passage? *Australian Journal of Outdoor Education, 8*(1), 29–36.

Bell, B. (2003). The rites of passage and outdoor education: Critical concerns for effective programming. *Journal of Experiential Education, 26*(1), 41–50.

Berry, J. (2006). Whose threshold? Women's strategies of ritualization. *Feminist Theology: The Journal of Britain & Ireland School of Feminist Theology, 14*(3), 272–288.

Cushing, P. J. (1998). Completing the cycle of transformation: Lessons from the rites of passage model. *Pathways: The Ontario Journal of Outdoor Education, 9*(5), 7–12.

Cushing, P. J. (1999). Translating transformation into something real. *Pathways: The Ontario Journal of Outdoor Education, 12*(1), 26–29.

Dalton-Puffer, C. (2007). *Discourse in content and language integrated learning (CLIL) classrooms.* Amsterdam: John Benjamins.

Dewey, J. (1997 [1938]). *Experience & education.* New York: Touchstone.

Gibbons, M. (1974, May). Walkabout: Searching for the right passage from childhood and school. *Phi Delta Kappan,* 596–602.

Grimes, R. L. (2000). *Deeply into the bone: Re-inventing rites of passage.* Berkeley, CA: University of California Press.

Houston, J. (1996). The initiation of Telemachus. In L. Mahdi, M. Meade, & N. G. Christopher (Eds.), *Crossroads: The quest for contemporary rites of passage* (pp. 35–40). Chicago: Carus.

Kehoe, A. B. (1997). *Humans: An introduction to four-field anthropology.* New York: Routledge.

Kornfield, J. (1996). Buddhist monastic initiation. In L. Mahdi, M. Meade, & N. G. Christopher (Eds.), *Crossroads: The quest for contemporary rites of passage* (pp. 41–51). Chicago: Open Court.

Maddern, E. (1990). What is it fifteen year olds need? *Horizons, 7*(1), 29–32.

Meade, M. (1996). Rites of passage at the end of the millenium. In L. Mahdi, M. Meade, & N. G. Christopher (Eds.), *Crossroads: The quest for contemporary rites of passage* (pp. 27–34). Chicago: Open Court.

Oldfield, D. (1996). The journey: An experiential rite of passage for modern adolescents. In L. Mahdi, M. Meade, & N. G. Christopher (Eds.), *Crossroads: The quest for contemporary rites of passage* (pp. 147–165). Chicago: Open Court.

Prazak, M. (2007). Introducing alternative rites of passage. *Africa Today, 53*(4), 19–40.

Somé, M. (1996). Ritual, the sacred, and community. In L. Mahdi, M. Meade, & N. G. Christopher (Eds.), *Crossroads: The quest for contemporary rites of passage* (pp. 17–26). Chicago: Open Court.

Suler, J. R. (1990). Wandering in search of a sign: A contemporary version of the vision quest. *Journal of Humanistic Psychology, 30,* 73–88.

Turner, V. W. (1969). *The ritual process.* London: Routledge & Kegan Paul.

Unsoeld, J. (1985). Education at its peak. In R. Kraft & M. Sakofs (Eds.), *The theory of experiential education* (2nd ed., pp. 108–122). Boulder, CO: Association of Experiential Education.

van Gennep, A. (1960 [1909]). *The rites of passage* (G. L. Caffee, Trans.). Chicago: University of Chicago Press.

van Wyk, G. (2002). Severance pain. *Geographical, 74*, 28–35.
Walsh, V., & Golins, G. (1976). *The exploration of the outward bound process.* Unpublished manuscript.

We are grateful for Rebecca Platz' early contributions to this chapter

Brent Bell
University of New Hampshire

Simon Beames
University of Edinburgh

Will Carlson
University of New Hampshire

TIM STOTT

5. SCIENCE ON EXPEDITIONS

A wheel mark in the desert lasts for decades. A footprint in the Arctic takes
years to fade. Yet the expeditions which make these marks may further our
knowledge of the world in which we live, helping us to conserve it... ...the
benefits of expedition science should outweigh the problems of disturbance.
Tipping the balance in the right direction depends on awareness and care during
the expedition, and publication of the results. (Macklin, 1991, pp. 40–41)

In the UK, there are now more organisations providing educational expeditions for
young people as school vacation or gap year experiences than ever before. Both
anecdotal evidence and now a growing body of systematic research evidence,
suggest that expedition experiences can develop knowledge, skills, and understanding
that can enhance a person's well-being and future employability. In this chapter,
we discuss expeditions that involve the measurement and collection of field data
and information from the expedition area - in other words the sort of work that is
now often described as "traditional" fieldwork.

Expedition members often undertake other activities such as investigations of
social interaction or behavior change (Forrester and Stott, 2009), artwork, making
videos, investigations of members' responses to arduous conditions and creative
writing. Whilst these may all be useful and worthy additions to an expedition
programme, they fall outside the scope of this chapter. Instead, the scientific
fieldwork being examined here is the sort that provides a unique opportunity to
learn about biological and geographical processes on the ground, where they are
happening. This type of fieldwork has seen a sharp decline over the last decade
(Smith, 2009).

HISTORY OF SCIENCE ON EXPEDITIONS

This section aims to show, by means of several examples taken over the past five
centuries, how many important research discoveries, findings and even theories
have been generated from conducting expedition-based scientific research.

Ferdinand Magellan (1480 – 1521) was a Portuguese maritime explorer who
was the first to lead an expedition across the Pacific Ocean and made the first
successful attempt to circumnavigate the Earth. Captain James Cook (1728 – 1779),
an English explorer, navigator and cartographer, achieved the first European
contact with the eastern coastline of Australia and the Hawaiian Islands, as well
as the first recorded circumnavigation of New Zealand in the 1770s. Charles
Robert Darwin (1809 – 1882) was an English naturalist, whose five-year voyage on

S. K. Beames (ed.), Understanding Educational Expeditions, 45–53.
© 2010 Sense Publishers. All rights reserved.

the Beagle allowed him to make geological and natural history collections, and to eventually conceive his theory of natural selection in 1838. Fridtjof Nansen (1861 – 1930), a Norwegian explorer, scientist and diplomat led the first crossing of Greenland by ski in 1888, and achieved great success with his Arctic expedition aboard the Fram, which in 1893 was deliberately allowed to drift north. But, after a year in the sea ice it became apparent that Fram would not reach the North Pole, so Nansen and Johansen started north on foot from 84° 4′ N on March 14, 1895 and three weeks later reached 86° 14′ N, the highest latitude then attained. During this first crossing of the Arctic Ocean, the expedition became the first to discover the existence of a deep polar basin and the first to note and describe dead water, a strange phenomenon which can occur when a layer of fresh or brackish water rests on top of denser salt water, without the two layers mixing.

Robert Falcon Scott (1868 – 1912), a British Royal Naval officer and explorer led two expeditions to the Antarctic regions: the Discovery Expedition (1901–04) and the ill-fated Terra Nova Expedition (1910–13). Scott's scientific crew included meteorologists, hydrologists, zoologists, glaciologists, biologists and geologists, all under control of Dr E. A. Wilson, the Chief Scientist. In the austral winter of 1911, Wilson led "The Winter Journey", a 60-mile journey in total darkness and temperatures down to –57 °C, with Bowers and Cherry-Garrard to the Emperor penguin breeding grounds at Cape Crozier to collect eggs for scientific study. Cherry-Garrard (1994 [1922]) later described this expedition in his memoir, The Worst Journey in the World. The following year Captain Scott led a party of five, manhauling their supplies, which famously reached the South Pole on 17 January 1912, only to find that they had been preceded by Roald Amundsen's Norwegian party in an unsought "race for the Pole". On their return journey Scott and his four comrades all perished because of a combination of exhaustion, hunger and extreme cold. The bodies of Scott, Wilson, and Bowers were discovered the following spring in their tent some 12 miles from One Ton Depot. Amongst their belongings were 35 lbs of geological specimens which had been collected on the moraines of the Beardmore Glacier. Over 1900 rock specimens from the expedition are housed at The Natural History Museum today. Of these specimens, many have given geologists evidence for continental drift, for example. Solomon and Stearn's (2001) The Coldest March, provides new information about the weather encountered by the polar party in February and March 1912, and makes the case that they were killed "not primarily by human error but by this unfortunate and unpredictable turn of meteorological events" (p. xvii). Perhaps because of the heroism and tragedy, but certainly because of the publicity and numerous books subsequently written (e.g. Roland Huntford and Ranulph Fiennes), Scott's Antarctic expeditions, one may argue, placed expedition-based scientific research onto the agenda of future expeditions and brought it into the public eye. Indeed, the late Surgeon Commander G. Murray Levick was a member of Scott's Antarctic Expedition of 1910–13, and in 1932 he founded BSES Expeditions (the British Schools Exploring Society), which is widely acknowledged as the first organisation to annually offer young people the opportunity to participate in expeditions to remote wilderness areas around the world. Today, BSES Expeditions is a well-established youth development charity offering spring, summer, and gap year expeditions to young people aged 16½ – 20. BSES expeditions still has a firm commitment to engage young people in scientific research while on expedition – a philosophy which has stood the test of time since Scott's expeditions.

This section of the chapter has shown that many important research discoveries, findings and even theories have been generated from conducting expedition-based scientific research. In some cases the expeditions have been voyages of discovery which have deliberately set out to be so, usually mapping and charting new coastlines, conducting hydrographical surveys and collecting specimens. Other expeditions have had specific geographical aims such as reaching a pole or summit, but have conducted scientific research into geology, meteorology, and physiology, for example, as part of the journey. In more recent times, some expeditions have specifically set out to discover what has happened to past expeditions such as Franklin's Lost Expedition to the Northwest Passage or to Mallory and Irvine on Everest. What then, can we learn from these examples taken from the past, which will help our understanding of educational expeditions? Well, if nothing else, that expeditions have been valuable means of exploring the world and improving our understanding of how it works, and perhaps what our past, present and even future impacts on it are likely to be.

SCIENTIFIC RESEARCH ON EXPEDITIONS TODAY

Scientific research on expeditions today lends itself to studies in the natural sciences in remote and inaccessible parts of the Earth far from communications networks (e.g. Stott & Grove, 2001; Stott, 2002). The expedition is used as a means of accessing that particular environment or problem. The research is normally carried out by researchers working in Universities or Government Research Councils or Research Institutes, but will often require a supporting team to help with logistics. However, investigations in remote regions can be conducted by anyone who is comfortable operating in the expedition environment. Graduates and undergraduates frequently undertake research on expeditions, perhaps to meet the requirements of their undergraduate projects or dissertations, Masters or PhD theses. Sometimes university students organise such expeditions themselves, though they are normally organised by or with university staff who conduct their own research, but may also supervise students who carry out projects. Such expeditions may be funded by universities themselves, by grants from research councils and/or charities, or students may raise funds themselves from sponsorship. These expeditions differ from those where young people essentially buy an expedition experience from a provider. This type of expedition experience may be purchased by a whole class in a school, or several schools may join to make a viable expedition group. The experience may be off-the-shelf or may be designed by the school teachers and expedition provider together. Thus, younger students (e.g. 14–16 years old) may also undertake research on expeditions that may be part of school projects at GCSE or A-level, or Duke of Edinburgh's Award. A few such Youth Expedition providers still include science as part of their programme.

Scientific research on expeditions may be subject-based and investigate, for example, a region's meteorology, glaciology, geomorphology, hydrology, geology, zoology or botany. In the past few decades questions about the impact of climate change and global warming have driven a great deal of research effort. This continues today and will almost certainly continue into the foreseeable future. Another type of research frequently carried out on expeditions is concerned with testing and evaluating such things as safety procedures, oxygen equipment, tents, clothing, medical procedures, communications, and transport systems. A third type of research on expeditions may be research on the expedition participants themselves. Some of this can be classed as scientific, such as physiological studies concerned with human adaptation to high altitude on mountaineering expeditions (Moore, 2000). Other investigations into the educational impacts of expeditions (Allison, 2002; Beames 2004a&b; Stott & Hall, 2003) are classed as education or social science research, while studies of expedition stress and personality-change (Watts, Webster, Morley, & Cohen, 1992; Watts, Cohen, & Toplis, 1994) would be classed as psychology.

Beames and Stott (2008) found that after a three month expedition young participants' responses identified a statistically significant improvement in their ability to plan and lead group projects; confidence in dealing with people from different cultures and countries; resilience to succeed when the "chips are down"; self awareness; and preparedness to influence group situations. Likewise, Stott and Hall (2003) found that participants in a six-week wilderness expedition in NE Greenland self-reported statistically significant changes in their ability to set priorities, achieve goals, solve problems efficiently, manage time efficiently, be enthusiastic, organise others, lead through consultation with others, demonstrate confidence and set goals - all skills required for, and enhanced by, undertaking systematic data collection in the field, which is one particular type of scientific research.

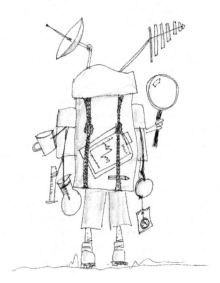

SCIENTIFIC FIELDWORK ON YOUTH EXPEDITIONS

Britain has more than 75 years of organised youth exploration that is largely aimed at providing adventure and challenge to young people. Most early youth expeditions carried out a significant amount of fieldwork, such as the surveying and mapping of glaciers, mountains and lakes in the traditions of geographical exploration. But today's expeditions have moved on. Contemporary professional scientific expeditions still aim to explore the challenges of climate change, functioning and conservation of fragile ecosystems, or the human impacts on diminishing resources. Youth expeditions, on the other hand, tend to show a decline in fieldwork in favour of adventurous activities or community projects.

Most schools and universities still recognise the value of fieldwork in their ecology, geography, earth and environmental science curricula (Andrews, Kneale, Sougnez, Stewart, & Stott, 2003; Lonergan & Andresen, 1998; Warburton, Higgitt, & Watson, 1997) as a means of gaining first-hand interaction with the real world, for learning field techniques used by researchers, and for students to conduct their own field-based investigations. Some would argue that expeditions provide an ideal platform from which to teach and learn about fieldwork (Smith, 2009). However, few of the increasing number of youth expedition providers still include traditional science and fieldwork in their programmes, with those that do tending towards the descriptive survey and mapping of landforms approach taken by early explorers, and only a few undertaking process-based fieldwork (i.e. fieldwork in which processes that occur in nature, such as the speed or movement of gravel in a river, are measured to further our understanding). Smith (2009) reports that "according to records kept by Geography Outdoors, the centre supporting field research, exploration and outdoor learning at the RGS-IBG, the proportion of youth expeditions undertaking field projects has fallen to one in ten" (p. 4). This may be due to the growth of commercial providers of expedition experiences who organise adventurous activities and community projects; they are seen to be "putting something back" into the host country, but do so at the expense of science and fieldwork. However, if commercial providers are responding to their clients' demands, it follows that the clients (usually school groups) may not be asking for science and fieldwork in their expedition programme - perhaps because it might be seen by students as "too much like school". However, if teachers do not ask for science and fieldwork to be included in the programme, its decline will inevitably continue.

A second factor may be the reduction in fieldwork provision in many schools and universities, fieldwork being costly and time consuming to provide and manage. As the impact of this reduction has fed through to the current generation of young adults, the resultant loss of fieldwork experience and expertise may have had an impact on teachers, expedition providers and volunteer leaders with the confidence to take on the responsibility for expedition field projects. A third factor has been the growth in popularity of adventurous activities in exotic locations. The appeal of kayaking, scuba diving or bungy jumping to potential expedition members is obvious, but these kinds of adventurous activity tend to focus on the personal growth and skills of participants rather than on the exploration of the world around them. That this may be happening at the same time that there is growth in numbers participating in youth expeditions means that the huge and growing potential for youth expeditions as an informal global classroom is perhaps not being maximised.

In the state education sector there now seems to be an increasing emphasis on the value of enrichment activities outside the classroom, reinforced in the UK by the government publication of a *Manifesto for Learning Outside the Classroom* and the appointment of Educational Visits Co-ordinators (EVCs) in schools and colleges. In light of the increasing popularity of youth expeditions, it would seem that youth expedition providers are ideally placed to make an important contribution to this education outside the classroom and also to embrace the national concern about the decline in fieldwork opportunities in schools and universities. Research into learning on youth expeditions suggests that expeditions are very effective for developing understanding, setting priorities, achieving goals, solving problems efficiently, managing time efficiently, organising others, leading through consultation with others, demonstrating confidence and setting goals (Stott & Hall, 2003; Beames & Stott, 2008). Perhaps most importantly, this research showed statistically significant changes in participants' self-reported enthusiasm, so that the biggest impact that expeditions could have would be to increase interest, motivation and an inclination to find out more about themselves, the people they are with, and the place they are in.

Following their expeditions, many young people go on to study related degrees in geography, earth, biological or environmental sciences or take up careers in geography, environmental sciences or conservation work after inspirational fieldwork experiences. So, youth expeditions can help to develop young people's field skills, reverse the decline in school and university fieldwork, and contribute to the next generation of field scientists and explorers. Expeditions can provide practical field experience such as animal and plant identification that expedition members may not be experiencing at school or university. Finally, and perhaps most importantly, there is the value of fieldwork in raising young people's environmental awareness. Often expeditions travel long distances to work in environmentally sensitive locations which can result in significant environmental cost. Such costs are now being measured in terms of ecological footprints or carbon tariffs. These can and should be mitigated to some extent by increasing the environmental awareness of expedition members, aiming to change the way that young people see and value the world. Well designed field projects (see Implications for Practice box) can increase understanding of environmental problems and lead to lifelong changes in values, attitudes and behaviour on the part of participants, which should, in the longer term, offset some of the environmental cost of the expedition.

CONCLUSIONS

A review of the history of scientific research on expeditions examines the early discovery voyages of Magellan and Cook, Darwin's voyage of the Beagle and Nansen's drift of the Fram to the North Pole. Scott's Antarctic Expeditions, the second famously ending in tragedy, nevertheless arguably contributed more to science than most, with geological specimens collected helping, many years later, with the theory of plate tectonics. Gino Watkins's expeditions in Greenland to collect meteorological data for the British Arctic air route planned from England to Winnipeg, collected valuable data which helped make transcontinental air travel a reality. Expeditions have been valuable means of exploring the world and improving our understanding of how it works, and what our past, present and future impacts on it are likely to be. Yet, despite this fact, Geography Outdoors (the RGS-IBG centre supporting field research, exploration and outdoor learning) reports that the proportion of youth expeditions undertaking field projects has fallen to one in ten (Smith, 2009).

Various reasons for this decline are discussed, not least the reduction in fieldwork in schools and universities. The UK government now seems to be placing an increasing emphasis on the value of enrichment activities outside the classroom, reinforced by its publication of a *Manifesto for Learning Outside the Classroom* and the appointment of Educational Visits Co-ordinators (EVCs) in schools and colleges. In the light of the increasing popularity of youth expeditions, it would seem that youth expedition providers are ideally placed to make an important contribution to this education outside the classroom, and also to embrace the national concern about the decline in fieldwork opportunities in schools and universities.

IMPLICATIONS FOR PRACTICE	
Fieldwork more likely to engage young people	*Fieldwork less likely to engage young people*
readily grasped and carried out	requires detailed conceptual understanding, specialised skills, or extreme precision
mapping boundaries such as vegetation, coastlines, glaciers or snowfields – particularly re-mapping features that may have been mapped by earlier expeditions to assess change	geological mapping
projects involving the identification of a controlled number of readily recognised species	plant physiology experiments
transects involving observation or sampling	serious surveying of terrain
mapping and determining land use, settlements, or agriculture	projects requiring anything other than simple taxonomic identification
measurement of environmental parameters with straightforward probes or meters, e.g. flow in rivers	projects involving interviewing local people where there is a language barrier

IMPLICATIONS FOR PRACTICE *(Continued)*

use of questionnaires	specific behavioural observations of readily observed animals
sampling that involves counting, cover estimation, biomass or simple diversity indices	most studies of landforms where no change can be observed within the timescale of the expedition (with possible exception of rivers, where changes during the expedition can usually be observed)
creating local maps for local use	ecological projects that require theoretical understanding
mapping or archaeological excavation	most projects requiring sophisticated equipment and instruments, and pointless and tedious collection of data

Adapted from Smith (2009)

DISCUSSION QUESTIONS

1. What can we learn from past expeditions which have carried out important scientific research which will help our planning and execution of educational expeditions today?

2. Why has "traditional fieldwork" on expeditions declined in favour of adventurous activities and community projects?

3. How can we reverse the reported decline in scientific fieldwork on youth expeditions?

4. How can expedition providers "sell" fieldwork to young people without it sounding like more school work?

5. How are skills gained by doing fieldwork on expeditions valuable or transferable to future careers and wider society?

REFERENCES

Allison, P. (2002). *Values, narrative and authenticity: A study of youth expeditions in the 1990s.* Unpublished PhD dissertation, University of Strathclyde.

Andrews, J., Kneale, P., Sougnez, Y., Stewart, M., & Stott, T. A. (2003). Carrying out pedagogic research into the constructive alignment of fieldwork. *Linking Teaching and Research and undertaking Pedagogic Research in Geography, Earth and Environmental Sciences*, Planet Special Edition 5, 51–52.

Beames, S. (2004a). *Overseas youth expeditions: Outcomes, elements, processes.* Unpublished PhD dissertation, University of Southampton.

Beames, S. (2004b). Critical elements of an expedition experience. *Journal of Adventure Education and Outdoor Learning, 4*(2), 145–157.

Beames, S., & Stott, T. A. (2008, March). Raleigh International pilot study report: Summary of findings on how participants were influenced by a 10-week expedition to Costa Rica. *Report presented to Raleigh International.*

Forrester, B. J., & Stott, T. A. (2009). Stop driving me wild!!! Does the wilderness experience influence archaeopsychic behaviours? *Journal of Qualitative Research in Sport Studies, 2*(1), 175–190.

Lonergan, N., & Andresen, L. (1998). Field based education: Some theoretical considerations? *Higher Education Research and Development, 7,* 63–77.

Macklin, D. (1991, July). Impact of expeditions: Footprints forever. *Geographical Magazine,* 40–44.

Moore, L. G. (2000). Comparative human ventilatory adaptation to high altitude. *Respiration Physiology, 121*(2–3), 257–276.

Smith, M. (2009). *Exploring a changing world: A guide to fieldwork for youth expeditions.* London: Young Explorers Trust.

Solomon, S. (2001). *The coldest march: Scott's fatal Antarctic expedition.* London: Yale University Press.

Stott, T. A., & Grove, J. (2001). Short-term discharge and suspended sediment fluctuations in the pro-glacial Skeldal River, NE Greenland. *Hydrological Processes, 15,* 407–423.

Stott, T. A. (2002). Bed load transport and channel bed changes in the proglacial Skeldal River, Northeast Greenland. *Arctic, Antarctic and Alpine Research, 34*(3), 334–344.

Stott, T. A., & Hall, N. E. (2003). Changes in aspects of students' self-reported personal, social and technical skills during a six-week wilderness expedition in arctic Greenland. *Journal of Adventure Education and Outdoor Learning, 3*(2), 159–169.

Warburton, J., Higgitt, M., & Watson, B. (1997). Improving the preparation for fieldwork with IT: Preparation tutorials for a remote field class. *Journal of Geography in Higher Education, 21*(3), 333–339.

Watts, F. N., Webster, S. M., Morley, C. J., & Cohen, J. (1992). Expedition stress and personality-change. *British Journal of Psychology, 83*(3), 337–341.

Watts, F. N., Cohen, J., & Toplis, R. (1994). Personality and coping strategies on a stressful expedition. *Personality and Individual Differences, 17*(5), 647–656.

FURTHER READING

Anker, C., & Roberts, D. (2000). *The lost explorer: Finding Mallory on Mount Everest.* London: Constable & Robinson.

Cherry-Garrard, A. (1994) [1922]. *The worst journey in the world.* London: Picador.

Fiennes, R. (1984). *To the ends of the earth: Transglobe expedition 1979–82.* London: Hodder & Stoughton.

Fiennes, R. (1993). *Mind over matter.* London: Mandarin.

Fiennes, R. (2003). *Captain Scott.* London: Hodder & Stoughton.

Huntford, R. (1979). *Scott and Amundsen: The race to the South Pole.* London: Dan Books.

Ridgeway, J. (1974). *Gino Watkins.* London: Oxford University Press.

Tim Stott
Liverpool John Moores University

PETE ALLISON AND KRIS VON WALD

6. CHOICES, VALUES, AND UNTIDY PROCESSES: PERSONAL, SOCIAL, AND HEALTH EDUCATION ON EDUCATIONAL EXPEDITIONS

In this chapter we want to explore the underpinnings of what happens on expeditions and to make connections between expeditions and educational aims with reference to the current educational climate in the UK. This discussion is an attempt to create a meaningful and useful focus for expedition leaders and providers by offering a conceptual framework for learning on expeditions.

EXPEDITIONS

When we talk about expeditions we are referring to experiences of a month and longer. Our experiences are with expeditions in the wilderness (the main mediums being science work and adventure); mountaineering expeditions in the greater ranges (to climb high peaks or to undertake journeys at altitude); and expeditions to developing countries (typically involving community work and adventure). The arguments we make in this chapter are not limited to these kinds of expeditions but we are using them as a frame of reference and a back drop for the discussion. We believe that leaders of shorter expeditions (such as Duke of Edinburgh Award expeditions) will also benefit from considering the issues explored and the implications for their practice.

It is also worth noting that much of the literature on expeditions and outdoor education assumes that young people are involved. Our experience is that increasing numbers of adults are interested in expeditions and adventures which involve learning. We believe that part of the reason for this growing interest and involvement in expeditions is that expeditions normally enjoy plenty of time for reflection with is a key part of experiential learning theory that is often overlooked in schools. However, in this chapter we draw on current curriculum in the UK and use examples of young people on expeditions.

LEARNING THROUGH EXPERIENCE

Our understandings and our preferences are as experiential learners and educators. Such a philosophy and approach to learning and education rests on assumptions that people learn best through experiences and that as educators we cannot dictate what people learn but rather create situations in which learning is likely to occur (DeLay, 1996; Dewey, 1938; Moon, 2004; Wurdinger, 2005). These are usually situations in which people are stimulated and intrigued by something – often a

S. K. Beames (ed.), Understanding Educational Expeditions, 55–65.
© 2010 Sense Publishers. All rights reserved.

problem or a challenge of some kind (hence there is a close connection between educational expeditions and problem and project-based learning). Our developing understanding of what happens on expeditions is based on fundamental principles of experiential education.

Expeditions have the capacity to become a community of practice (Lave & Wenger, 1991), and so it should follow that learning can occur not just for the participant, but also for leaders, assistant leaders and all involved in an expedition. This is a point which, as far as we understand, is somewhat overlooked. If learning is not occurring for everyone – and in our experience learning invariably is taking place for all involved – then we might sensibly ask questions regarding the philosophy of the leaders and the pedagogical (children's learning theory), andragogical (adults' learning theory), ethical and moral environment of the expedition.

It is a further and very different question to ask how and when learning is taking place. Sometimes learning is enjoyable and an immediately enlightening process. At other times learning is difficult, painful and often not realised until well after the event. This is part of the benefit of the length of time involved in and the intensity of expeditions – it allows teaching, learning and breakthroughs to happen in their own time. Expeditions are not constrained by the same kinds of time pressures that are often present in shorter outdoor education experiences.

VALUES AND HEALTHY CHOICES

Education is concerned with values (Allison & Wurdinger, 2005; Allison, 2000a&b; Carr, 2000, 2003; Carr, Allison & Meldrum, 2006). Whether through the subjects taught, the way they are taught or who teaches them – values are implicit in the whole process. Likewise, expeditions live and breathe values from the organisations, the leaders, the young people, the costs, the destinations and the activities, to name but a few. Indeed, it is hard to gain any meaningful comprehension of expeditions without a values framework of some kind. All of these values are inherent in the choices made. Accepting that expeditions are couched in values is not particularly new or indeed controversial. However, we want to suggest this emphasis on values is placed much more front and centre than it has traditionally been and is currently. In other words, conceptualising expeditions as a moral endeavour is our first suggestion and assumption, and the starting point for our discussion is choices and decisions.

We all have to make choices in our lives every day. Some choices are small (what to eat) and others are larger (what kind of job we want to have) and a large part of growing up and becoming a member of society is about developing our abilities to make choices – and preferably "good" ones. Furthermore, some choices appear small and may be large and vice versa. Deciding what to eat can be a big choice as it demonstrates our values – how we treat our bodies, others and the environment. We ask if the food is good for us, from a sustainable source, or organic, in order to make three of the most obvious choices that face us in a supermarket (which also demonstrates how our values are reflected in the places where we may choose to shop).

Making choices and decisions requires us to weigh up options and balance out the advantages of different courses of action, which requires thinking and considering the processes and outcomes of various pathways. When decisions need to be made about serious things they usually require some deliberation—they are rarely straightforward—and are not normally measured on one scale, but more typically through a complex tapestry of multi-dimensional scales. In *Ethical Issues in Experiential Education,* Hunt (1990) offers a seminal overview and discussion of these complexities from an ethical perspective in the context of experiential learning. These options, it can be argued, are ways in which we are empowered as consumers and more generally as individuals in society with increasing degrees of autonomy and self determination.

Awareness of the range of options that are open to us as moral agents introduces another important idea. This is the diversity of options available and the recognition that other people select different options from ours – that is to say that other people express different preferences through the choices they make. The more that we become aware of such differences the less can be assumed or taken for granted. While we might still select the same options when we are faced with choices, we can see them in a different light and recognise that they are not the only or the *right* options. Although much more can be said on the issue of choices and values, the intention here is to sketch over the territory in order to make the point that these are centrally important ideas for moral agents to engage with, and ones that are, we believe, unavoidable on expeditions.

PERSONAL, SOCIAL, AND HEALTH EDUCATION (PSHE) AND OUTDOOR EDUCATION

Outdoor education is a general term describing a number of fields of practice which are often associated with PSHE, PSD (personal and social development) and related terms. Our experience of talking to people is that PSD is often understood as developing confidence, cooperation, trust and teamwork. Talking with people working in the field of outdoor education suggests that self esteem is regularly identified as central to PSD. Readers interested in conceptual and practical understanding of self-esteem are advised to read Kristjánsson (2007a&b). In his insightful work he criticises the social science conception of self esteem. The author cites the lack of correlation between low global self esteem and relevant educational variables as good reason to focus on domain-specific self esteem which is chiefly concerned with school subjects and students self-respect. Notwithstanding debates on the nature and measurement of self esteem we believe that developing appropriate self concept or self awareness is a more helpful way of identifying what is often the *raison d'etre* of expeditions.

In some publications, PSD is taken to be synonymous with problem-solving. This is illustrated in an early publication (Payne, 1984) by the *National Association for Outdoor Education* (now morphed into the *Institute for Outdoor Learning*) titled *The Outdoors and Personal Development,* which is a compendium of problem solving initiative games. In the introduction Payne states,

> 'Games' provide an opportunity to set up adventurous situations which will involve the group in problem solving, decision making, working as a team, taking responsibility for themselves and one another in comparative safety. (p. 3)

No further explanation of how this happens and how activities are connected to PSD is offered other than some brief discussion of the importance of a three stage process (teaching aims, adventure games, review and reflection). Further publications have developed ideas of PSD and outdoor education in a range of ways. Almost ten years after the above publication Hopkins and Putnam (1993) produced *Personal Growth Through Adventure,* which remains a popular text with many students. More recently the office for standards in education in England and Wales (Ofsted) produced the report *Outdoor Education: Aspects of Good Practice* (2004) which encourages a link with PSD and states that "the strength of this work is significant in students' personal development but it is not yet an integral part of the formal curriculum" (p. 13).

One further publication is worthy of note at this stage. In 2006 a report from a two-year study of values and character formation in the 21st century was published in which the following comment was made:

> Activities such as residential trips, the Duke of Edinburgh scheme and students organising their own clubs, societies and discussion groups are instrumental in developing character, virtue and values. (Arthur, Deakin-Crick, Samuel, Wilson & McGettrick, 2006, p. 113)

Although we have identified a few landmark publications we believe to be influential and of particular interest rather than complete an exhaustive literature review on the broad subject of PSD, this sets the general stage in the field of outdoor education and allows us to focus more specifically on the expeditions sector.

It is worth noting that there has been a recent change in terminology and PSD has been replaced by PSHE, which is becoming more fashionable in the UK. This change may illustrate an interpretation of health in a narrow or strict sense as health promotion and fitness, which has seen numerous political initiatives in recent years. Readers may be interested in *The Health Impacts of the John Muir Award* (Mitchell & Shaw, n.d.), which uses a broader conception of health – referring to healthy, positive and conscious choices, decisions and taking responsibility. It is the latter and broader conception that we prefer and believe to be relevant to outdoor education generally and expeditions specifically.

PSHE AND EXPEDITIONS

In the UK expedition field (which has seen considerable growth since the early 1990s) PSHE has been integral to taking young people on expeditions, often overseas. This is based on a first assumption that expeditions have some connections to education (albethey often informal). A brief look at marketing materials and web sites of expedition organisations illustrates that much of the terminology used is borrowed from mainstream education and suggests, overtly or covertly, that taking part in an expedition will have some educational benefits. Sometimes this means, for example, that taking part in an expedition will help to gain access to university and at other times increase the likelihood of obtaining employment as it will "look good" on a Curriculum Vitae. This is all very well but it is difficult to find much more detail on how and why this might happen. Similarly, this appears to be the case in schools.

In the National Curriculum (Qualification & Curriculum Authority, 2009), which is taught to all students in state schools in England and Wales up to the age of 16, students do not study PSHE but do study foundation subjects in Religious Education (RE) and Citizenship. It is also statutory that students are taught careers education and sex education. Further, there are two non-statutory programmes of study in secondary school: Economic and Financial Capability (careers education, work-related learning, enterprise and financial capability) and Personal Well-being (which covers sex and drugs education and Social and Emotional Aspects of Learning (SEAL)).

On examining this area it is immediately evident that it lacks a clear educational policy. Indeed, Haydon (2005) has addressed this issue specifically, noting that the difficulty of identifying PSHE as a subject contributes to its low profile. He suggests that Citizenship is essentially concerned with social morality and our responsibilities to other citizens, and that RE focuses on religious aspects of the ethical environment. Crucially, however, he argues that PSHE should be able to

...enable them [individuals] to take an overview of the whole range of values impinging on their lives, to help them find an orientation and direction and to give them some basis for the choices they have to make. Without such an overview, they may be missing some of the important features of the very environment on which their choices depend. (Haydon, 2005, p. 31)

CURRICULUM FOR EXCELLENCE

In Scotland, *Curriculum for Excellence* is taught in all state-funded schools up to the age of 18 and aims to develop four overarching capacities: successful learners, confident individuals, effective contributors to society and responsible citizens (Learning & Teaching Scotland, 2009). This is a relatively new curriculum (implemented in 2008–9) and one in which PSHE falls between social studies, health and well-being, and religious and moral education. On reviewing literature and observing emerging practice as the new curriculum is phased in, it quickly becomes clear that Haydon's concerns in England and Wales are even more relevant in Scotland. The increasing fragmentation of issues typically associated with PSHE is a cause for concern and it seems unlikely that young people will be supported in taking the overview of influences that Haydon refers to above.

While on expedition it is easy to imagine a young person in radically different situations, with new challenges and other people from different places, while facing the enormity and beauty of nature and the wilderness. Often, expedition experiences are happening at crucial times in life (teens) when metaphysical (rather than empirical) questions dominate. These factors make it difficult for young people to avoid asking "who am I?" and similar humbling questions as transcendental, aesthetic and spiritual issues often come to the fore. For example, the start of an expedition is often the first time young people have had to introduce themselves to others who have no idea of who they are. In doing so they must consider: Who am I? Who are you? How do I want to introduce myself to you? What is my history? What is interesting about me? What is interesting about you? What is different about us? What is similar about us?

Significant learning is often found in noticing what is different (Bateson, 1972). There are often rich opportunities on expeditions to consider what it might be like to live here and to be part of this culture and the beliefs and values of local people. Participants and leaders can examine taken-for-granted assumptions about their own values and beliefs which can, in turn, inform their own attitudes and behaviour.

Given the gap which Haydon (2005) so astutely identifies in current curriculum provision in Great Britain, it seems that the role of PSHE on expeditions may be of great importance. Expeditions may be able to contribute to filling this gap in peoples' lives and thus contribute to their growth, learning, and ultimately, to them living well-balanced, considered and contented lives. We believe it is useful to think about PSHE on expeditions as concerned with developing awareness of, and offering opportunities to, explore values and choices as individuals and groups. This can lead to a greater understanding of self, enhanced abilities to develop relationships with others, and recognition of healthy values, choices and relationships.

LEARNING ON EXPEDITIONS

Linking this discussion regarding learning, choices and options to learning on expeditions can be done in at least two ways. First of all we can think about an expedition in which there are no choices. We can try to imagine what it might be like to plan and implement an expedition that involves no choices for young people and perhaps even leaders too. It is hard for us to imagine such a scenario, but in trying to do so an image of a highly autocratic structure comes to mind and a community environment that is not very stimulating. Second, we can imagine an expedition where there are endless choices to be made by young people and leaders "in the field". Such an environment conjures up an image of a rich (and perhaps untidy) learning environment where ideas are discussed (often passionately), people are happy and sad, excited and disappointed and experiencing a range of other emotions.

Most expeditions fall somewhere between these two hypothetical systems and represent varying opportunities for leaders and young people to make choices. We believe this is a good thing as such choices can create opportunities for exploring values, consequences of actions and responsibility for choices. It also creates an environment where all of those who are involved in expeditions – young people, leaders and the provider organisations – are exposed to the implications of their choices and learning opportunities.

DECISIONS

If young people are expected to make choices that are meaningful rather than contrived, then mistakes are inevitable. In order for young people to be able to make choices on expeditions that may result in mistakes, they need encouragement. They also need support to know that it is acceptable, and even desirable, to make mistakes. In order to gain some confidence in making choices it is normally helpful at first for leaders to create small opportunities with a few options and to make the expectations explicit. Such situations must be as genuine as possible – contrived situations are normally "seen through" by young people – either at the time or subsequently. It also goes without saying that choices and decision making need to occur within a framework of acceptable safety (physical, emotional, and spiritual). Opportunities for choices can then be developed and bigger opportunities created with more complex decisions and preferences required.

A favourite example of creating structures to encourage choice involves a group on a canoe expedition in Africa. When they set out one morning they went in entirely the wrong direction. The two leaders followed along, as the group were in charge. When the group realised their mistake that evening there was some heated and extensive discussion. The following day they retraced their journey to be back at their starting point after a 48 hour sojourn. Needless to say, they did not make the same mistake again and have dined out on the story numerous times since! This example illustrates how leaders can place learning (through experience) centrally and prioritise this over the tempting lure of doing things right and reaching a destination. The experience of making mistakes brings up group issues of how choices are made, who is responsible for decisions and the consequences of the decisions, and the leaders' role in decision making. These are all areas for individual and collective learning that can be part of an educational expedition when elements of choice for participants and leaders are included.

LEADERS AND LEADERSHIP

We believe that experiences and situations requiring choices and exploring values need to occur with an understanding of group process and leadership. Early on in an expedition individuals might be given responsibility for leading a part of a journey where there are route choices to be made, decisions on speed and time for breaks. As the days progress, individuals might make choices regarding where to camp and for how long until, in time, groups may be responsible for agreeing on choices over several days of where to walk and set up camp, speed, timing and more while leaders may be shadowing from a distance. On some expeditions a system of "leader for the day" is operated where one participant is allocated to lead the group for the day. This may be a helpful starting point but seems to rest on some assumptions regarding leadership such as (i) one person can be responsible for all decisions throughout a day; (ii) all people aspire to be leaders and; (iii) a contrived situation such as this somehow results in leadership development.

We prefer a more fluid system where individuals and groups are given increasing levels of responsibility, whereby they can explore issues such as preferred roles, skills, context and shared decision making. As this already happens on some expeditions some readers may be wondering what is new here. Our suggestion is that this is central to the expedition and provides an organising framework for planning and understanding the expedition experience for all who are involved.

Leaders on expeditions are generally given the responsibility for "teaching" young people in some way. Little attention has been paid to the learning involved in expeditions for leaders. At the beginning of the chapter we discussed learning through experience and the value of experiential education. We believe that through the experience of expeditions it seems inevitable that there are opportunities for leaders to learn. By creating a learning community in the expedition, the exchange between leaders and young people does not have only one direction. It would be hard to imagine how even a skilled, experienced, and wise leader would emerge from an expedition unscathed by the experience of exploring values, knowing the consequences for actions, and taking responsibility for choices.

Our experience and understanding is that if young people are to make choices (and mistakes) then leaders can, and we believe should, also make choices and have appropriate levels of responsibility. In order to do so they need to have sufficient latitude and support from the organisations they are working for to make choices – often explicitly discussing such choices with young people – and in doing so can set an appropriate climate for choices, mistakes and learning to take place. However, this requires a certain amount of flexibility and scope within the expedition in order to allow for certain timing, direction and distance choices to be made on the ground and not completely planned in advance. This can be uncomfortable for the provider organisation where certainty is highly valued, but good communication systems in the field can alleviate uneasiness back at the base. This also requires leaders to be capable of transcending their egos (or at least keeping them in check) and being comfortable in their role as leader, choice maker, mistake maker, and above all else, as a learner on the expedition alongside the young people (Raab, 1997).

All of the above raises questions regarding how people are developed or grown to become "sound leaders" who can work in the ways described above. In mainstream education this aspect of teaching is normally referred to as professionalism or professional practice and requires at least a minimal understanding of ethical issues associated with teaching and learning and educational theory. This is an area for further work and development if it is to become a realistic proposition and catch up with the increasing need for leaders in the expedition sector.

A CONCEPTUAL FRAMEWORK FOR LEARNING ON EXPEDITIONS

If all of the above were to be in place on an expedition and choices were to be used as an organising framework, a whole host of further issues emerge which will need to be addressed. Leaders, in particular will have to be skilled and willing to work within such a structure, and leaders and young people will have to be prepared to take some risks with regard to choice taking. Perhaps most importantly, leaders will have to be prepared to work with uncertain outcomes, each other, and young people to create an environment on the expedition where learning from choices is prioritised and valued in practice. In order for choices to be made and learning to be included, discussions regarding these choices and considerations of consequences and implicit values may be appropriate. This creates endless opportunities to explore the learning prior to, during and subsequent to making choices.

All involved in expeditions need to be willing to place learning at the centre of the experience, along with the aim of increasing understanding and engaging with, and "mapping", the ethical landscape. Such a process has potential to be stimulating and to enrich people's lives. Furthermore, an educational conceptualisation of expeditions leads to a rich learning experience which helps all people involved to learn from various elements of science, adventure, other people similar to themselves, other people radically different from themselves and, of course, the literal, moral, spiritual and ethical environment.

OUTCOMES

Like all forms of education it is important that expeditions are thought through and the aims and objectives are considered with care. Each expedition ought to have well considered and developed philosophies and rationale for what is being done, where, when and with whom. It is important to contemplate what is to be achieved before starting anything. That is not, of course, to say that plans need to be detailed in prescriptive learning outcomes that squash opportunities for creativity, flexibility (for choices to be made), and making the most of a "teachable moment".

Whether in a classroom, far off land, community or wilderness, leaders (teachers) must consider their aims and issues when choosing where to go, what to do and how to do it. Readers interested in this issue may find the seminal work of Hirst & Peters (1970) useful in exploring key conceptual, curricular and educational issues. More recent work by Carr (2000; 2003) may also be of interest.

Payne (1975) argued that expeditions have two objectives: a stated objective (e.g. climbing a mountain) and a hidden objective (e.g. what each individual on the expedition hopes it will provide for them). He suggests that the more congruence between these objectives, the more successful the expedition will be. Payne concluded,

> ...if expeditions are going to help people achieve a satisfactory personal and emotional identity they must be so organised that the participants have an opportunity of taking responsibility or exercising leadership and of doing a number of things without supervision. This may be less tidy and it may to some extent diminish the smooth running of an expedition, but if the objects of the expedition are not endangered and no–one's life is put at risk, in my opinion this is an essential part of the maturation which expeditions...should seek to encourage as actively as possible. (p. 5)

Anyone who has even a little experience of teaching understands that learning is not normally a "tidy" process. This applies to the learning on expeditions, and maybe even more so because the "classroom" is not easily controlled. However, knowing that the learning may be untidy is not an excuse for a lack of consideration for the learning aims and objectives that are possible given the location, duration, group and timing of an expedition.

CONCLUSION

We believe expeditions provide ideal opportunities for people to engage in learning through experience, and indeed that learning on expeditions is unavoidable. The educational value of the expedition can be connected to the current educational climate in the UK (and probably elsewhere without much difficulty) as articulated through the principles of PSHE and *Curriculum for Excellence*. Gaining an understanding of values through choices and decisions that young people, leaders and organisations make before, during and after expeditions is inevitable when the conceptual framework includes this type of learning as its foundation.

Knowing that learning is at the centre, carefully planned expeditions provide the right environment for all who are involved to gain positive experiences that contribute to their personal growth and development.

IMPLICATIONS FOR PRACTICE

– Personal, Social, and Health Education (PSHE) is a complex and often misused term but one which is central to meaningfully understanding expeditions. PSHE is concerned with exploring values and making healthy decisions based on values and principles.

– Expedition leaders and planning organisations that claim to be developing people in this area will offer higher quality expedition experiences if they gain some understanding of values education, the perspectives of young people and learning processes. Conceptualising their work in this way and maintaining an ongoing discussion of the values that they are promoting is important in developing practice that is coherent with their stated aims, values, and benefits.

DISCUSSION QUESTIONS

1. What are the barriers to PSHE occurring on expeditions?

2. What can expedition leaders do to nurture the learning environment on an expedition?

3. How could expedition leaders/staff organise the days and weeks of the expedition in such a way they revolved around the theme of choices and values?

4. How can leaders be developed to work effectively in the conceptual framework outlined in this chapter?

REFERENCES

Allison, P., & Wurdinger, S. (2005). Understanding the power, promise and peril of the experiential learning process. *Teacher Education and Practice, 18*(4), 386–399.

Allison, P. (2000a). Constructing values: An expedition case study. In P. Barnes (Ed.), *Values and outdoor learning* (pp. 159–167). Penrith, NSW: AfOL.

Allison, P. (2000b). *Research from the ground up: Post expedition adjustment.* Cumbria: Brathay Hall Trust.

Arthur, J., Deakin-Crick, R., Samuel, E., Wilson, K., & McGettrick, B. (2006). *Character education: The formation of virtues and dispositions in 16–19 year olds with particular reference to the religious and spiritual.* Pennsylvania: The Templeton Foundation.
Bateson, G. (1972). *Steps to an ecology of mind.* New York: Ballantine Books.
Carr, D. (2000). *Professionalism and ethics in teaching.* London: Routledge.
Carr, D. (2003). *Making sense of education.* London: Routledge.
Carr, D., Allison, P., & Meldrum, G. (2006). In search of excellence: Towards a more coherent Scottish common school curriculum for the twenty-first century. *Scottish Educational Review, 38*(1), 13–24.
DeLay, R. (1996). Forming knowledge: Constructivist learning and experiential education. *Journal of Experiential Education, 19*(2), 76–81.
Dewey, J. (1938). *Experience and education.* New York: Macmillan.
Haydon, G. (2005). *Impact No. 10. The importance of PSHE: A philosophical and policy perspective on personal, social and health education.* Macclesfield, UK: Philosophy of Education Society of Great Britain.
Hirst, P. H., & Peters, R. S. (1970). *The logic of education.* London: Routledge.
Hopkins, D., & Putnam, R. (1993). *Personal growth through adventure.* London: David Fulton.
Hunt, J. (1990). *Ethical issues in experiential education.* Boulder, CO: Association for Experiential Education.
Kristjánsson, K. (2007a). Justified self-esteem. *Journal of Philosophy of Education, 41*(2), 247–261.
Kristjánsson, K. (2007b). Measuring self-respect. *Journal for the Theory of Social Behaviour, 37*(3), 225–242.
Lave, J., & Wenger, E. (1991). *Situated learning: Legitimate peripheral participation.* New York: Cambridge University Press.
Learning & Teaching Scotland. (2009). *Curriculum for excellence.* Retrieved June 10, 2009, from http://www.ltscotland.org.uk/curriculumforexcellence/curriculumoverview/aims/fourcapacities.asp
Mitchell, R., & Shaw, R. (n.d.). *Health impacts of the John Muir Award.* Retrieved June 10, 2009, from http://www.gcph.co.uk/content/view/165/68/
Moon, J. (2004). *A handbook of reflective and experiential learning.* London: Routledge Falmer.
Ofsted. (2004). *Outdoor education: Aspects of good practice: HMI 2151.* London: Crown.
Payne, J. A. (1975). Well being on expeditions. *YETprint, 8*(5/6), 1–5.
Payne, S. (1984). *The outdoors and personal development.* Occasional Publications: No. 1. Penrith, NSW: National Association for Outdoor Education.
Qualifications & Curriculum Authority. (2009). *National curriculum.* Retrieved June 10, 2009, from http://curriculum.qca.org.uk/
Raab, N. (1997). Becoming an expert in not knowing: Reframing teacher as consultant. *Management Learning, 28*(2), 161–175.
Wurdinger, S. (2005). *Using experiential learning in the classroom: Practical ideas for all educators.* Lanham, MD: Rowman & Littlefield.

The authors would like to thank Peter Harvey, Kristjan Kristjánsson, and Ed Raiola for their helpful comments on earlier versions of this chapter.

Pete Allison
The University of Edinburgh

Kris Von Wald
Independent Consultant

MORTEN ASFELDT, GLEN HVENEGAARD, AND INGRID URBERG

7. EXPEDITIONS AND LIBERAL ARTS UNIVERSITY EDUCATION

People have always needed to learn the skills required to live well in the world, yet formal schooling is a relatively new phenomenon. While the intentions of much organized education are laudable, there are limitations and drawbacks. For example, common disciplinary divisions are often a product of administrative efficiency rather than sound pedagogy; seating students in rows and using lectures as the normal teaching method is sometimes a product of large classes and faculty desire; discouraging field trips and other types of off-campus learning is often driven by high cost and the fear of litigation. However, before the advent of formal schools, people learned how to survive and thrive by solving the problems that faced them on a daily basis; problems that arose from their lived experience and resulted in real consequences. Finding solutions for these set a foundation for further learning. Educational expeditions provide such opportunities in a university curriculum, and while we do not advocate the end of formal education, we do suggest that university-based educational expeditions acknowledge the shortcomings of institutionalized education, and are an attempt to return to a more intuitive, organic, and natural form of learning.

Today, educational expeditions are found in many universities, serve a vast array of objectives, and include travel to all parts of the globe. These expeditions are sometimes for academic credit and other times not; sometimes a program requirement and other times optional; sometimes led by full-time faculty but also by contract staff or guest professors; and serve students, faculty, and universities in numerous ways. For many students, it is a sought-after form of learning, and an opportunity to learn about the world and themselves. For faculty, it is a chance to engage students in a holistic manner that is difficult in the classroom. And for universities, it is an important means of attracting students, expanding their network of connections, and at times, generating funds. In recent years, the popularity of wilderness orientation programs, which assist new students in the transition from high school to university, has grown dramatically (Bell, Holmes, & Williams, in press).

This chapter will provide a brief overview of the wilderness educational expeditions at the University of Alberta's Augustana Campus. We will explore the role of educational expeditions in the liberal arts and sciences today (hereafter referred to as the liberal arts), identify key findings and trends from the related literature, and examine a number of common expedition themes.

S. K. Beames (ed.), Understanding Educational Expeditions, 67–78.
© 2010 Sense Publishers. All rights reserved.

EDUCATIONAL EXPEDITIONS IN THE LIBERAL ARTS

Educational expeditions in universities today come in many forms, and address a myriad of objectives. These expeditions vary in length from a weekend to several months and are offered by a wide variety of disciplines. In some cases, students also receive academic credit for completing expeditions from organizations such as Outward Bound and the National Outdoor Leadership School.

The goals of university expeditions are also varied. They include, for example, personal growth, leadership development, disciplinary-specific skill development and knowledge acquisition (e.g. outdoor, research, historical, geographical, biological, writing, and language) cultural awareness, community development, environmental sustainability, and spiritual exploration. Due to their holistic nature, educational expeditions fit well within a liberal arts education.

For some time, a liberal arts education has been threatened and overshadowed by the utilitarian nature of vocational and professional training, which is more focused on job-related skills. However, primarily smaller undergraduate universities and colleges continue to offer a liberal arts education. For example, our institution's goal (Augustana, n.d.) is to educate "the whole person in an intimate, small-campus setting so that students and mentors alike are capable of engaging life with intellectual confidence and imaginative insight, equipped for leadership and service, and committed to the betterment of their world" (para. 3). David Orr (1991) recognizes the contributions of liberally educated people in claiming the world needs "more peacemakers, healers, restorers, storytellers, and lovers of every shape and form. It needs people who live well in their places. It needs people of moral courage willing to join the fight to make the world habitable and humane." (para. 16). Orr also feels that "modern curriculum[s] have fragmented the world into bits and pieces called disciplines and subdisciplines…[and] most students graduate without any broad integrated sense of the unity of things" (para. 14).

While a liberal arts education has been criticized by some for lacking utilitarian value, university and college educations have been criticized more generally for the absence of, and sometimes an outright disregard for, sound pedagogy and teaching practice (Epp, 1999; Pocklington & Tupper, 2002). In response to such concerns, and in an attempt to improve undergraduate teaching, Chickering and Gamson (1987) developed seven principles that have been widely accepted as good practice in undergraduate education: encouraging contact between students and faculty; developing reciprocity and cooperation among students; encouraging active learning; giving prompt feedback; emphasizing time on task; communicating high expectations; and, respecting diverse talents and ways of learning.

While these practices are being applied in some classroom settings, educational expeditions, by their nature, lend themselves toward their implementation. Of these practices, Kuh, Pace, and Vesper's (1997) research identifies faculty-student contact, cooperation among students, and active learning as particularly important predictors of student educational gains in college. These principles are particular strengths of educational expeditions where students and faculty live, learn, and travel together for extended periods; where cooperation among students is required for the process of living, learning, and travelling together; and, given the holistic and immersive nature of educational expeditions, active learning is the norm.

In this light, educational expeditions fit well into a liberal arts education because they have the potential to address disciplinary fragmentation, engage students in pedagogically sound learning experiences, and prepare students for a life well-lived. As Chickering and Gamson (1987) point out, "an undergraduate education should prepare students to understand and deal intelligently with modern life" (para. 10).

CURRENT LITERATURE

While theoretical and descriptive literature is plentiful in the field of outdoor education, empirical research on educational expeditions is sparse, particularly on university-based expeditions. Nevertheless, the growing body of pedagogical and outdoor education literature is helpful for planning and implementing educational expeditions. Here is a brief overview of three relevant empirical studies.

Beames (2004) studied elements of an overseas youth expedition that influence participant outcomes. (While not a university-based expedition, the results are helpful nonetheless). He identified five critical elements of the expedition experience: group isolation (constant company of group members), changing groups (changing groups after three weeks), diverse groups (heterogeneous versus homogenous group composition), physically demanding (being challenged physically), and self-sufficient living (experiencing independence in daily living, such as cooking, sleeping, and cleaning).

Daniels (2005) studied the life significance of a spiritually oriented wilderness expedition at Montreat College, North Carolina, USA. The most significant components of the wilderness program were the solo experience (37%), rock-climbing (15%), and teamwork (15%). The solo was important since it provided opportunities for solitude, challenge, reflection, and interaction with God. While solos are not part of all educational expeditions, educators should consider the role of any expedition's novelty, timing, challenge, spiritual influence, perspective, and setting.

Finally, Paisley, Furman, Sibthorp, and Gookin (2008) identified five mechanisms through which students learned the National Outdoor Leadership School curriculum (i.e. outdoor skills, leadership, risk management, expedition behavior, communication, and environmental ethics). These mechanisms were structure-oriented (built into the course by instructors), instructor-oriented (instructors' teaching techniques), student-oriented (student actions which are independent of the instructors), student-and-instructor oriented (lessons learned from student and instructor actions), and environment-oriented (learning from immersion in the environment). Technical skills (e.g. outdoor, risk management, and environmental ethics) were generally learned through instructor-oriented and student-oriented mechanisms, while process-oriented skills (e.g. leadership, expedition behavior, and communication) were generally learned through environment-oriented, student-oriented, and structure-oriented mechanisms.

In summary, these findings can help educators plan an expedition's learning objectives and program mechanisms. While the specific literature in this area is sparse, much can be learned from the broader fieldwork literature in disciplines such as medicine, geography, and biology (Bonello, 2001; Keller, 2005; Kent, Gilbertson & Hunt, 1997). In addition, research opportunities are plentiful.

CENTRAL THEMES IN UNIVERSITY WILDERNESS EXPEDITIONS

Here we will focus on select themes from two specific outdoor education expeditions offered on the University of Alberta's Augustana Campus: a 21–day summer canoe expedition in the Canadian Arctic (see Hvenegaard & Asfeldt, 2007a) and a 14–day winter dogsled expedition in the Canadian sub-arctic (see Asfeldt, Urberg, & Henderson, 2009). These expeditions differ from other educational travel and exchanges offered by Augustana, as they are entirely self-sufficient, though some of the themes discussed are shared by other educational expeditions, travel, and exchanges at Augustana.

Leadership Development

Kurt Hahn was among the first outdoor educators to use adventure as a means for leadership development. Describing Outward Bound (OB), Hahn says:

> [OB] was not started to teach people how to live in the mountains but to use the mountains as a classroom to produce better people, to build character, to instill intensity of individual and collective aspiration on which an entire society depends for its survival. (James, 2008, p. 109)

While Hahn does not use the term "leadership" here, his description of OB is consistent with current themes in the broader leadership literature (e.g. Bennis, 2004; Kouzes & Posner, 2002; Wheatley, 1999) and our rationale for incorporating educational expeditions in the liberal arts.

By analyzing traditional outdoor education perspectives on leadership (Martin, Cashel, Wagstaff, & Breunig, 2006; Priest & Gass, 2005) within the broader leadership literature, it appears leadership in the outdoor education field is more about management and skill competence than true leadership. Kouzes & Posner's (2002) extensive and long-term research involving leaders from around the world, and from diverse settings, identify being honest, forward-looking, competent, and inspiring as the four characteristics most expected of leaders. Similarly, Bennis (2004) suggests that direction, trust, and hope are what followers seek in leaders and that trust is the pivotal characteristic. Again, Bennis claims that "[t]imeless leadership is always about character, and it is always about authenticity" (p. xxiv). These examples reflect commonly revealed themes, which point to leadership being about relationships, self-awareness, vision, values, character, and credibility. Overall, then, leadership development, at its core, is about self-development, much like the essence of a liberal arts education.

Often, the focus of outdoor leadership programs is outdoor skill development (and also often the most sought after by students). Driven by our support for the liberal arts, we strive to balance our provision of holistic leadership development opportunities with outdoor skill development. For us, our educational expeditions are a means to an end rather than an end in itself, where the end is a liberally educated person whose leadership skills are transferable beyond the outdoor setting and form a foundation for a life well-lived.

Outdoor Skill Development

While skill development is not our primary goal, it is important. Many of our students go on to work as wilderness guides and outdoor skill instructors - and do it well - and students learn the basic skills of wilderness living and travel (e.g. canoeing, backpacking, navigation, Leave No Trace) in an introductory outdoor education course which is a pre-requisite for all our subsequent outdoor education expeditions. As well, we assist students in further developing specific outdoor skills in preparation for each unique expedition. Furthermore, in order to graduate, outdoor education students must obtain three certifications, including wilderness first-aid, one instructor certification (e.g. canoeing, kayaking, skiing) and one safety certification (e.g. river rescue, avalanche safety). Therefore, in spite of our emphasis on holistic leadership development that we see as central to a liberal education and the foundation for becoming an outstanding leader, outdoor skill development remains an important aspect of our programs and wilderness educational expeditions can be an effective means for their development.

Connecting to Nature and Place

People are becoming increasingly disconnected from nature and place. We often see this disconnection manifested in, for example, our students' ignorance of aspects of the natural world that sustain our lives (e.g. water, food, shelter, and heat). Sadly, this disconnection affirms Leopold's (1949) claim that a modern person "is separated from the land by many middlemen, and by innumerable physical gadgets. He [sic] has no vital relation to it" (p. 223). Leopold labeled this disconnection "landlessness". We believe that this state of landlessness contributes to many current environmental, cultural, and social maladies. One of the many goals of our educational expeditions is to create a sense of "landfullness" (Baker, 2005) in our students by re–establishing a vital relationship to nature and place, which may then encourage them to play more active and responsible roles in shaping their local and global landscapes. To this end, we encourage and lead students in the discovery and knowing of nature and place.

Like other outdoor educators, we do this in many ways. For example, in teaching the *Geography of the Canadian North*, we use the mode of a 21–day wilderness canoe expedition. As the group lives and travels together, we, as instructors, demonstrate our passion and knowledge for species, ecosystems, human impacts, and a land ethic. We hold our students accountable for increasing their own knowledge by requiring intensive study of the natural and cultural history of the expedition region, by way of written assignments, field research studies, identification tests, student interpretive talks, and personal journals. Our goal is to develop in students the processes and frameworks for gaining and retaining knowledge of the land, which can also be applied in all geographic regions of their lives. Such knowledge is the foundation for understanding and appreciating the significance of these landscapes and provides an impetus for becoming personally involved in decisions regarding the future of these landscapes.

In another course, *Explorations of the Canadian North,* personal narratives are used to connect to nature and place, and students spend the first six weeks analyzing personal narratives from the expedition region. This prepares students for immersion into the place and demonstrates how others have come to understand their own experiences of that place. We also discuss how these stories reflect Canadian history and culture more generally. In addition, these narratives offer examples of how students may analyze and write about their own expedition experiences and provide a method to explore other expedition goals (e.g. leadership development, personal growth, group dynamics). Professors and students then spend 14–days in an isolated sub–arctic environment, with six days on a dogsled expedition and eight days studying at a remote wilderness homestead. Later, through writing workshops, students produce personal narratives of their expedition experiences.

Many educational benefits are derived from combining wilderness travel with reading and writing personal narratives. First, "the outdoor experience gives students something immediate and deeply felt to write about" (Bennion and Olsen, 2002, p. 241). Second, the art of story-telling and an awareness of our own stories are enhanced in the process of reading and writing personal narratives, which in turn contributes to leadership development and connections to nature and place. For Baldwin (2005), story "connects us with the world and outlines our relationship to everything" (p. 3). Finally, the discipline of literature provides students with the tools to understand, tell, and write stories and narratives. Gruenewald (2003) believes that the two processes of reading the world and reading the word actually reinforce each other, rather than eliminate the need for the other. This supports Dewey's belief (1929) regarding the need for both primary (hands–on) and secondary (reflective) components of any truly educational experience.

Interdisciplinarity

Narrow disciplinary approaches to undergraduate education have become the norm in most North American universities (Hvenegaard & Asfeldt, 2007b; Klein, 1990; Pocklington & Tupper, 2002). However, there is growing recognition that an emphasis on interdisciplinary education can open up new ways of knowing, and broaden the types of questions pursued and methods employed (Lattuca, 2001). Lattuca claims that there is no difference between a liberal education and an interdisciplinary education and that interdisciplinarity is not a new idea but rather an old idea that has become popular in response to the fragmentation resulting from disciplinary division. Klein (1990) defines interdisciplinarity as "the use of more than one discipline in pursuing a particular inquiry" (p. 27) and for Bunting (2006) it means, "that more than one discipline…is woven into the learning experience with the objective of realizing their connections" (p. 14). Using Dewey's (1938) terminology, we propose that interdisciplinary learning requires the use of knowledge, theories, and ideas of multiple disciplines to render an indeterminate situation determinate and to fully understand the experience of living.

Given our setting in a liberal arts university, our expedition practices reflect our goals of deeply understanding and connecting to place and nature, coupled with our desire to see students develop genuine leadership skills for a life well-lived. Ultimately, we want students to view their educational expedition experiences through many different disciplinary lenses so they may gain a fuller understanding and perspective of their areas of study, themselves, and each other.

Reflection

One aspect of experiential education that sets it apart from other educational philosophies is the necessary practice of reflection (Joplin, 2008). Thus, we include many such opportunities (both formal and informal; private and public) in our programs.

Our more formal methods of reflection include a personal journal, group journal, and facilitated discussions and debriefings. The use of personal journals in our programs has been influenced by the writing of Christina Baldwin (1991) and her belief that a journal meant to promote personal growth and awareness should remain private unless willingly shared. Therefore, we guide students through a self-evaluation process of their journals.

The group journal has become a highlight of our journeys and has taken many forms (e.g. prose, poetry, song, art, and humor). In the group journal process, each member of the group (including instructors) takes turns making a daily entry that is read aloud to the group the following morning. This type of journal plays an important role in group formation and bonding, and requires students to make public, and hence assume accountability for, their experiences and reflections (Priest & Gass, 2005). We have found that both personal and group journals are an important means for students to integrate, explore, and articulate various disciplinary perspectives, new understandings, and observations. The group journal also serves as a springboard for further inquiry, discussion, and learning.

A third method of formal reflection is through instructor- and student-led discussions and debriefings. During these times together, we address many issues: from the basics of travelling and functioning as a group, to decision-making and the exploration of difficult or controversial issues and behaviors. This method is also used as a place for giving and receiving feedback on such topics as peer leadership.

Informal methods of reflection and interaction include time spent paddling, dog-sledding, hiking, cooking, journaling, and exploring together and alone. Other examples are talking with tent and cabin mates, and participating in the informal and fun banter that accompanies shared meals and living together in close quarters for an extended time - a unique and powerful element of educational expeditions. On expeditions, there are frequent unstructured opportunities for discussion and meaning-making, which are rare in typical university classroom and office settings and are strengths of wilderness educational expeditions. These are times of spur-of-the-moment discovery, where students can freely engage the land and each other.

CHALLENGES AND PITFALLS

In spite of the many benefits of educational expeditions, there are various challenges and pitfalls that may reduce their effectiveness and make their implementation difficult. Educational expeditions can be expensive for both students and universities. For students, there is the cost of travel, personal equipment, and lost wages during the summer. For universities, there are also costs for travel, equipment, administration, and faculty workload. These costs are perceived to be particularly significant if the expeditions involve small classes. There are also unique time commitments for both students and faculty. Educational expeditions necessitate time away - sometimes during the summer and sometimes during a regular school semester. In either case, for students it means lost wages or time away from other classes. For faculty, it means time away from families, regular teaching duties, or summer research time.

There are many forms of resistance associated with educational expeditions. This is sometimes felt from other faculty members who are asked to accommodate students who miss classes during the semester; from university administrations who must free up faculty time and other resources to offer expedition-based courses; and from students who are sometimes more interested in the adventure than embracing academic components of expeditions such as formal reflection, processing, and assessment activities.

IMPLICATIONS FOR RESEARCH

There are many opportunities for future research associated with educational expeditions. For example, investigators might clarify and compare critical elements of university expeditions that promote learning; examine the role of university expeditions in student dynamics (e.g. retention, satisfaction, choice of majors, and career decisions), evaluate the level of congruence among student, instructor, and institutional objectives for university expeditions; expand interdisciplinary research that addresses the dynamics and results of university expeditions. Such research could integrate the perspectives of many disciplines including, for example, economics, geography, history, sociology, education, and modern languages and literatures.

Further research might also examine how consistent the central themes for wilderness university expeditions are for expeditions with diverse objectives, student groups, geographic locations, travel modes, and formal activities. Researchers could also assemble a list of best practices associated with different types of university expeditions and examine theoretical concepts, methodological approaches, and best practices found by other disciplines in the context of fieldwork, experiential learning, and applied learning.

CONCLUSIONS

At the heart of a liberal arts and sciences education is the goal of preparing people to live well in the world. In this quest, educational expeditions have the ability to provide rich learning experiences that address common shortcomings of university teaching. While the research regarding university educational expeditions is scant, research from other disciplines and teaching pedagogies can inform educational expeditions.

Educational expeditions can be powerful and rewarding experiences for both students and instructors. At the same time, all educational expeditions are unique and can address many different themes based on the mission of the university, program goals, and instructor passions and skills. In our case, we use educational expeditions as an opportunity to develop leadership skills by facilitating self-development, re-establishing vital relationships to nature and place, helping to integrate disciplines, and promoting insights through formal and informal reflection.

Finally, educational expeditions incorporating sound pedagogical practices signal a return to a more natural form of learning that is often sought after by students and instructors. Furthermore, the interdisciplinary nature of educational expeditions, in which students and instructors live, learn, and travel together for extended periods of time, mirrors the interdisciplinary nature of life itself, and facilitates student learning in their preparation for a life well-lived.

IMPLICATIONS FOR PRACTICE

– Educational expeditions have the ability to address traditional criticisms and shortcomings of university education. However, educational expeditions must have clearly developed objectives that are aligned with institutional and programs goals.

– Educational expeditions lend themselves to the implementation of sound pedagogical practice. Nevertheless, instructors must be intentional about program structure and methods in order to maximize learning.

– Educational expeditions have the potential to promote unity and connections between disciplines and serve as excellent preparation for a live well-lived.

DISCUSSION QUESTIONS

1. From a pedagogical viewpoint, examine the benefits and constraints associated with university expeditions. Consider the perspectives of students, instructors, and their institutions.

2. Describe some key differences in teaching and learning between university expeditions and traditional classrooms.

3. University expeditions have evolved considerably in recent years. Speculate on how they will evolve in the future, considering, for example, changes in costs, student interest, new technologies, constraints on travel, and more.

4. From an ethical perspective, is it justifiable to use the fossil fuels required to travel to remote places?

REFERENCES

Augustana Campus Website. (n.d.). *About us*. Retrieved August 21, 2009, from http://www.augustana. ualberta.ca/aboutus/

Asfeldt, M., Urberg, I., & Henderson, B. (2009). Wolves, ptarmigan, and lake trout: Critical elements of a northern Canadian place–conscious pedagogy. *Canadian Journal of Environmental Education, 14*, 33–41.

Baker, M. (2005). Landfulness in adventure-based programming: Promoting reconnection to the land. *Journal of Experiential Education, 27*(3), 267–276.

Baldwin, C. (1991). *One on one: Self-understanding through journal writing* (Rev. ed.). Lanham, MD: Evans.

Baldwin, C. (2005). *Storycatcher: Making sense of our lives through the power and practice of story*. Novato, CA: New World Library.

Beames, S. (2004). Critical elements of an expedition experience. *Journal of Adventure Education and Outdoor Learning, 4*(2), 145–158.

Bell, B. J., Holmes, M. R., & Williams, B. G. (in press). A census of outdoor orientation programs at four-year colleges in the United States. *Journal of Experiential Education*.

Bennis, W. (2004). *On becoming a leader*. New York: Basic Books.

Bennion, J., & Olsen, B. (2002). Wilderness writing: Using personal narratives to enhance outdoor experience. *Journal of Experiential Education, 25*(1), 239–246.

Bonello, M. (2001). Fieldwork within the context of higher education: A literature review. *British Journal of Occupational Therapy, 64*(2), 93–97.

Bunting, C. (2006). *Interdisciplinary teaching through outdoor education*. Champaign, IL: Human Kinetics.

Chickering, A. W., & Gamson, Z. F. (1987). Seven principles for good practice in undergraduate education [Electronic Version]. *The American Association of Higher Education Bulletin, 39*(7), 3–7.

Daniels, B. (2005). The life significance of a wilderness solo experience. In C. E. Knapp & T. E. Smith (Eds.), *Exploring the power of solo, silence, and solitude* (pp. 85–102). Boulder, CO: Association for Experiential Education.

Dewey, J. (1938). *Logic: The theory of inquiry*. New York: Holt, Reinholt and Winston.

Dewey, J. (1929). *Experience and nature*. La Salle, IL: Open Court.

Epp, R. (1999, Spring). The call of the university. *Journal of Curriculum Theorizing*, 47–61.

Gruenewald, D. (2003). The best of both worlds: A critical pedagogy of place. *Educational Researcher, 32*(4), 3–12.

Hvenegaard, G., & Asfeldt, M. (2007a). Embracing Friluftsliv's joys: Teaching the Canadian north through the Canadian wilderness travel experience. In B. Henderson & N. Vikander (Eds.), *Nature first: Outdoor life the friluftsliv way* (pp. 168–178). Toronto, ON: Natural Heritage Press.

Hvenegaard, G., & Asfeldt, M. (2007b). *Integrating outdoor education and geography: Using experiential wilderness travel in the Canadian North*. Paper presented at the Being in Nature: Experiential Teaching and Learning Conference, Gisna Valley, Norway.

James, T. (2008). Sketch of a moving spirit: Kurt Hahn. In K. Warren, D. Mitten, & T. A. Loeffler (Eds.), *Theory and practice of experiential education* (pp. 105–115). Boulder, CO: Association for Experiential Education.

Joplin, L. (2008). On defining experiential education. In K. Warren, D. Mitten, & T. A. Loeffler (Eds.), *Theory and practice of experiential education* (pp. 16–23). Boulder, CO: Association for Experiential Education.

Keller, H. W. (2005). Undergraduate research field experiences: Tree canopy biodiversity in Great Smoky Mountains national park and Pertle Springs, Warrensburg, Missouri. *Council on Undergraduate Research Quarterly*, 162–168.

Kent, M., Gilbertson, D. D., & Hunt, C. O. (1997). Fieldwork in geography teaching: A critical review of the literature and approaches. *Journal of Geography in Higher Education, 21*(3), 313.

Klein, J. L. (1990). *Interdisciplinarity: History, theory, and practice*. Detroit, MI: Wayne State University Press.

Kouzes, J. M., & Posner, B. Z. (2002). *The leadership challenge* (3rd ed.). San Francisco: Jossey-Bass.

Kuh, G. D., Pace, C., & Vesper, N. (1997). The development of process indicators to estimate student gains associated with good practices in undergraduate education. *Research in Higher Education, 38*(4), 435–454.

Lattuca, L. R. (2001). *Creating interdisciplinarity: Interdisciplinary research and teaching among college and university faculty*. Nashville, TN: Vanderbilt University Press.

Leopold, A. (1949). *A Sand County almanac and sketches here and there*. New York: Oxford Press.

Martin, B., Cashel, C., Wagstaff, M., & Breunig, M. (2006). *Outdoor leadership: Theory and practice*. Champaign, IL: Human Kinetics.

Orr, D. (1991). What is education for? Six myths about the foundation of modern education, and six new principles to replace them [Electronic version]. *Context: A Quarterly of Humane Sustainable Culture, 27*, 52–59.

Paisley, K., Furman, N., Sibthorp, J., & Gookin, J. (2008). Student learning in outdoor education: A case study from the National Outdoor Leadership School [Electronic Version]. *Journal of Experiential Education, 30*(3), 201–222.

Priest, S., & Gass, M. A. (2005). *Effective leadership in adventure programming* (2nd ed.). Champaign, IL: Human Kinetics.

Pocklington, T., & Tupper, A. (2002). *No place to learn: Why universities aren't working.* Vancouver, BC: UBC Press.

Wheatley, M. J. (1999). *Leadership and the new science: Discovering order in a chaotic world.* San Francisco: Barrett-Koehler.

Morten Asfeldt, Glen Hvenegaard, and Ingrid Urberg
University of Alberta, Augustana Campus

BOB HENDERSON

8. UNDERSTANDING HERITAGE TRAVEL: STORY, PLACE, AND TECHNOLOGY

And then there is a feeling. It starts out small – so small that you're not even
sure what you are feeling. And it grows into something that stirs a
cosmopolitan of emotion. … you know that you have been a part of
something special, a secret that no one else can truly understand. But the
secret is not my own – it was shared with me; it is the secret of the lake.
Everything we were amazed by as our voyage pressed on, everything that we
saw and admired and took pictures of, existed long before we came, and will
prevail long after our departure. The tendency to get so caught up in our own
worlds makes us forget that other worlds exist even within our own planet.
Entire ecosystems outside of the one in which I live are born, raised and
eventually perish under the very same blanket of life that our Earth provides.
The serenity of this knowledge and the appreciation I developed for this
world is something I will not soon forget. As I lay back in our canoe that
night, a calm swept over me like something I can never remember feeling.
I like to think that it was my spirit acknowledging the secret that the lake had
shared with me.

Student Journal, Final Entry
Stephanie Will, 2008

"The secret of the lake": I have read hundreds - and I do mean hundreds - of
similar expressions that search for an understanding of the deeper implications of
nature-based, self-propelled, place-conscious, story-rich, technologically-simple,
travel education experiences. Simply put: educational expeditions with a heritage
travel focus. Each outstanding expression from a student journal is individual and
special, but there are patterns. I have collected particular patterns that express
moments of personal and cultural insights for over twenty-five years (Henderson,
Schrader, and Roebbelen, 2009). One can learn aplenty from collecting and
reflecting on student travel journals over time. This is the process used in part to
distil an understanding of story, place, and technology as vital components to
understanding heritage travel.

The secret of the lake: it is a vague statement at best. I'm not sure what is meant,
but I am sure it was a charmed personal insight with cultural implications. I am also
certain that the "learned behaviour" expressed here is not that of the urban/schooled
environment. Educational expeditions in remote wild settings [read: settings that
easily bare authenticity to an earlier time] can advance a holistic, expansive

S. K. Beames (ed.), Understanding Educational Expeditions, 79–89.
© *2010 Sense Publishers. All rights reserved.*

curriculum for personal and cultural discovery. Conventional schooling is all too easily compromised in this regard. I am reminded of education reformer / activist Derrick Jensen's (2004) epigram: "schools are not about knowledge acquisition, so much as being about learned behaviours" (p. 5). Jensen's learned behaviour of schooling denotes a hidden curriculum that is rarely addressed by educators. Educator Chuck Chamberlin (1994) captures the hidden curriculum well. He writes:

> The hidden curriculum embedded in those [teacher/guide-student] roles and relationship enhances or constrains their creativity; promotes either cooperation and solidarity within the classroom [or travel] community or individualistic competition; nourishes self-direction or dependence; contributes to an internal locus of control or to the expectation that powerful others will shape most personal and social decisions; offers growth of the whole child socially, emotionally, and spiritually or focuses more narrowly on knowledge and rationality; and a host of other consequences. (pp. 10–11)

Unlike conventional school environments, educational expeditions are well-placed to shape self-concepts, promote co-operation, nourish self direction, contribute to an internal locus of control and, among still further qualities, offer growth of the whole person. Heritage travel aims to elicit insights to earlier times while shedding light on current cultural practices. As educator, Sean Park (2007) has said: "our culture has shaped, and has been shaped by a narrow curriculum of success that does not reflect our need to live well in our places" (p. 52). The heritage travel curriculum can reflect our need to live well in our places. We might explore our role as native to the place (indigenous), and colonizer (with the related cultural contradictions), and activist (working for the place).

Story, place, and technology have a lot to do with the overall expression of joy captured in the "secret of the lake" comment. With the group travel experience[1] there is the land, the people, the readiness of the student, and the circumstances of the travel. The guide cannot affect these to a great extent. However, the approach – the way the land is greeted by us humans is the domain of my influence and intent. Heritage travel has a different orientation from conventional schooling, adventure travel, or environmental field trips. Adventure and environmental objectives are distinct. Challenge, skill development, and teamwork are typical hallmarks of adventure-based programmes, whereas interaction with local ecology and increased environmental awareness are common features of field studies courses. Despite heritage travel sharing these goals, it places its primary attention on story, place, and technology. Although this chapter addresses each of the three themes in turn, in practice they are a cultural exploration that is experienced in an integrated, seamless manner.

James Neill (2008) proposes a systematic framework for understanding outdoor educational experiences. He suggests that our central attention might be developed towards the individual, environmental themes, the activity, programming issues, the group, the instructors' role, and cultural considerations. All of these realms of attention are represented in educational expeditions to varying degrees of intensity and each realm represents a possible curriculum focus. Heritage travel is particularly attentive to cultural exploration.

The cultural realm asks us to explore what we can learn about our culture during and after our travel. It asks what, how, and why change might be experienced in ourselves and society. In experiential education generally, agency, belonging, and competencies are primary aspirations and powerful forces for learning (Carver, 1993). Agency is concerned with our ability to be self-determined or empowered to act on convictions (or indeed, even to have convictions). Belonging involves relationships with other people and to places. To belong is to feel connected and necessary. Competencies refer to the skills acquired to be a safe traveller and a wise citizen who can dwell well in our places. Given our current relationships with global and local ecologies, competencies must involve change to the status quo or a "critical pragmatism" over those forces preserving the status quo (Cherryholmes, 1998, pp. 151–152). Critical pragmatism commands humans to understand that they must change themselves in order to seek a viable consciousness. Preserving the status quo both environmentally and socially is no longer an option. The cultural realm in education today must involve "...an enlightenment in which the meanings of actions, both of one's own as well as of others are made transparent... For the guide it is to afford people a new means of self comprehension and thereby to interject new possibilities into their lives" (Fay, 1975, p. 80).

In heritage travel, we explore the present through attention to cultural practices of the past. There will be nationalistic sentiments of retracing travel routes used by indigenous peoples, explorers and pioneers in a celebratory spirit. There will be contradictions to ponder within these celebrations, acknowledging the treatment of indigenous peoples and the land by colonial ancestors. Mostly there will be an embodied understanding of, say, the fur trade, through the work of canoe travel, by dreaming into the life vision of a rock art painter of hundreds of years ago, and from considering loggers' industry in an old growth forest. Remember, an expansive curriculum is possible. In all cases, whether addressing celebration and/or guilt in association with heritage, there can be a powerful spirit of being part of a greater enterprise in life. This spirit is the site of new means of self-comprehension and possibilities.

Heritage travel moves beyond the conventions of hard and soft skill development in adventure travel and the environmental knowledge acquisition of environmental field experiences. Granted, these may be important qualities, but they demand different primary qualities, in terms of Neill's (2008) framework for outdoor education. Hard and soft skill development puts attention primarily towards the group cohesion and individual and group skills. Both of these attentions fall under inherently limited notion of bonding social capital (Beames & Atencio, 2008, p. 102) Important to heritage travel are warm skills – how we meet the place of travel and living, and green skills – our interpretative and communicative ability with place (Henderson, 2001). Warm skills involve our manners, so to speak, as inhabitants: how we perceive ourselves in the world and how we act as dwellers in a home environment. Green skills focus on our understanding of how the world works (natural world in the main, as well as people acting in the world). Beyond knowledge acquisition, green skills are communicative acts within the natural world and with others. When considered together, warm and green skills encompass the outward-looking relational development to others - be they other communities or those in other times and space. This has resonance with another kind of social capital, called bridging social capital, which can more readily broaden identities (Beames & Atencio, 2008, p. 102).

One's socio-cultural network can also be expansive. Horizons can be imaginatively stretched. Wildlands can be met warmly as a home-place where we communicate as community members. This is a grand environmental adventure for the inner self and as cultural work. It is assumed here that bonding within one's group is a first step toward social and environmental bridging and engagement. Moving beyond our narrow self to a more participatory consciousness (Berman, 1984) is an adventure as we consider a cultural reconciliation with our wider ecological communities. I believe that Whitehead (1967) would accept this as an adventure of ideas for the evolving twenty-first century. He wrote in 1933:

> But, given the vigour of adventure, sooner or later the leap of imagination reaches beyond the safe limits of the epoch and beyond the safe limits of learned rules of taste. It then produces the dislocations and confusions marking the advent of new ideals for civilized effort. A race preserves its vigour so long as it harbours a real contrast between what has been and what may be, and so long as it is nerved by the vigour of adventure beyond the safeties of the past. Without adventure, civilization is in full decay. (p. 279)

To make no mistake about it, heritage travel is about the present. It is about rendering the past as a felt experience: feeling the stories of the place viscerally with the romance they provide, but also with an exposure to the tensions that exist in the stories. This is a learned adventure all too often undermined in the non-experiential abstracted milieu of traditional schooling and the focused attentions of adventure and environmental education.

As a practitioner, I try to look at the outdoor travel educational experience/ expedition in its entirety; I partake, observe, reflect, and guide the experience as a whole, while deliberately neglecting the tendency to compartmentalize learning into categories of self/group/other or travel/personal and social development/ environmental awareness. Neill's (2008) cultural realm advances a more holistic treatment. Then again, one who seeks to understand educational group phenomena as a whole is perhaps fooling oneself. Maybe it has taken me three decades of categorizing to be able to put forward a more holistic effort! I'm not sure. I do, however, agree with Joseph Meeker's (1974) contention that a "hopeless attempt to see things whole is at least as worthy as the equally hopeless task of isolating fragments for intensive study, and much more interesting" (p. 12).

And so, in an effort to see things whole over time, I suggest that story, place, and technology are central to educational expeditions, yet generally are addressed peripherally. Heritage travel has the capacity to draw out these qualities of understanding centrally. They might look like another set of compartmentalized thoughts, but they exist together, as one.

The forms of agency, belonging, and competency so important to experiential education and the outdoor travel experience are those linked to story, place, and technology. One does not secure agency from a heritage travel perspective without a solid development in the maturation of story, where "how we make our experiences into story determines how we live our personal lives" and how there is an understanding "that stories connect us to the world and outlines our relationship to everything" (Baldwin, 2005, p. 3) One does not get belonging without place. Belonging to a home-place, and to one's group as home, is the conventional "belonging". But there is a widening of place and time consciousness with "the mobility of travel to explore connectedness to multiple landscapes" (Cuthbertson, Heine, & Whitson, 1997, p. 74). Finally, one does not get competency without an understanding of the forces of technology in our lives, where technology is a practice linked directly to culture (Franklin, 1990, p. 15).

STORY

The anthropologist Edward Said (1993) has stated that "Nations are narratives" (p. xiii). This means, of course, that they are a story that should be understood as a set of stories. The same is true of people. In outdoor experiential education circles it has been said many times, in many ways, that people live storied lives. We understand ourselves and others from the story sharing, identity creating process of simplifying the inner complexity of our lives. Stephanie's "secret of the lake" is a simple and rich idea with which to frame a set of stories that can draw out the complexity of learning.

Inherent in "the secret of the lake" comment is a mindscape that has been made expansive. Perhaps regarded by some as an empty place, through our travel the land and water may begin to echo with meaning. As we travel we learn about the logging history and efforts to extract massive pine trees via waterways; the native rock art drawn into the lake shore cliffs hundreds or thousands of years ago; the fishing lodges turned holiday camps with the advancement of acid rain pollution in the 1950s – 1970s; the surveyors, present day hunters, and fellow canoe trippers. They are all part of the story of the place. We become a part of the story of the place, too, and the place becomes part of our story. The stories of the past place and reflections on the future within a dynamic present make us time travellers of sorts: an important factor in being place travellers. There can be a resonance that gives meaning and joy to the stories we learn and make our own. Novelist Douglas Coupland (1991) has expressed the shift from empty to echo wisely: "Either our lives become stories or there is no way to get through them" (p. 5). We become more and more engaged as we move from empty to echo - empty self to echoing self, from an empty place to echoing place.

The secret of the lake is a story setting. Openings, plot, characters, time and endings all offer a *story making* and *story learning* quality. We are living and learning in profound ways – in primary and primal ways – when we are in experiences that involve life story making and life story learning. In heritage travel-based educational expeditions the educator designs curriculum and individual experiences so that we may each become "storiers" who are learning about ourselves in community and with others in time.

PLACE

When places are empty, and thus largely devoid of story, they are merely space. As Yi Fu Tuan (1977) notes, "Undifferentiated space becomes place as we get to know it and endow it with values" (p. 6). In other words, space is unstoried place. In experiential learning terms, places are sites of our agency, belonging, and competence. Place is mostly about belonging, and we belong when we are place-making and place-learning.

We all exist in places - be they our childhood bedroom or the cosmos. A simple and complex question is, How big is your "place"? The answer depends largely on your experience and your learning. It is possible to pass through spaces without them becoming place. Adventure travel with its particular primary focus towards personal and social/group development can readily encourage the notion of space-based, generalized travel. Place-based travel encourages the local context of the region (Baker, 2008; Brookes, 2002). So the nature of the experience is central, but so too is one's imagination. The poet Wallace Stevens (1942) has written that imagination "… enables us to live our own lives. We have it because we do not have enough without it" (p. 150). If the imagination is made great by experience in place, then one's place is expanded. Remember, curriculum can be expansive. Novelist James David Duncan (1985) calls a place-conscious intelligence a *native intelligence*,

> since it evolves as natives involve themselves in this region. Non-natives awake in the morning, in a body, in a bed, in a room in a building, on a street, in a county, in a state, in a nation. Natives, by contrast, awake in the centre of a little cosmos - or a big one, if their intelligence is vast - and they wear this cosmos like a robe. They sense the barely perceptible shifting migrations, moods and machinations of its creatures, its growing green things, its earth and sky. (pp. 53–54)

I am remembering Gus on our last day of travel on McArthy Bay. The day was calm and canoeists were quiet. From the bow on the canoe Gus admonished, "Hey Bob, it all looks like this doesn't it?". Confused, I responded somewhat quizzically, "Huh?". Then Gus blew me away with his imaginatively wise leap: "I mean all the blue and green on the Canadian maps – most of it all looks like this. I never knew that". Gus had connected not just to McArthy Bay, but to the Canadian Shield that comprises close to two thirds of the Canadian landscape. I assume that this was an imaginatively rich, place-conscious moment for him. I assume it helped him both understand and move beyond Margaret Atwood's claim from a convocation address in 1983 at the University of Toronto that "Nature is no longer what surrounds us, we surround it, and the switch has not been for the better" (para. 12). It was a "secret of the lake" moment.

TECHNOLOGY

Technology has come to be understood as new and improved commodities and systems, such as iPhones, wireless internet, hybrid automobiles, and carbon-fibre canoe construction. The problem with this understanding is that it narrows our conception of technology by significantly negating relevant "earlier" technologies and technological systems. The guitar around the campfire and the wood canvas canoe are two obvious examples. They are technology too. In conversation with Canadian philosopher Neil Evernden in the mid 1990s, he shared with me his view that "technology has become the knack of organizing Nature so we don't have to experience it". The wilderness lover in me worries that this is painfully true. The outdoor educator in me is convinced it is, and thus provides a further imperative for educators to respond with curricula where nature is experienced. This is a technological issue.

To complement the above, another Canadian philosopher George Grant (1969) noted a proliferation of technology as a new, improved quality. He referred to "intimations of deprival" (p. 139) as a means of capturing the idea that we are good at acknowledging what we get with new technology, but are much less aware of what we are giving up. In heritage-focused travel, we are often giving back to folks what is lost. There can be charmed emancipatory euphoria in this return to simpler, more direct, burdensome, and engaging technologies. The "secret of the lake" comment gains comprehension here. An example to attend to all of the above is needed.

When guiding educational expeditions, be they at a base camp or on the trail, I always ensure that there is an evening sing-song/story sharing circle around the wood stove "hearth" or outdoor campfire. There are no iPods, cell phones, or rows as in a classroom with some externally prescribed purpose. Here, the purpose is interaction, conviviality, and comfort. We will get closer and closer to the heat source as the evening wears on, and closer and closer to each other in the process. Interaction through activity and discussion, in pairs and with the whole group, are all blended together. There will be annoying smoke rising that forces minor shifting adjustments here and there, perhaps. As the fire light dims, it affects the selection of song and story and interaction. There is no convenient, clean, safe, ubiquitous surrounding central air or central flick of a switch luminous source. With these campfires, though rarely acknowledged, there is a joy of labour, a joy of common free purpose, and a joy of connecting means and ends. We cut and hauled and tended to our heat and light source ourselves. Means and ends connected. Sounds simple, but connecting means and ends is a rare occurrence in urban existences where technological advances move us further from nature's sources. Take the flick of the light switch as an example, or replace the campfire guitar sing-song with a boom-box radio for background.

Our travel is self-propelled. It can be hard work. Our food is cooked communally and eaten together. It takes care and time. By comparison to our conventional daily urban-schooled lives, the travel and campfire life is burdensome. Yes, undoubtedly - but it is engaging. The corollary to Evernden's assertion of our distance from nature is that we can now be disburdened from Nature (Strong, 1995, pp. 80–87). Our modern lives have offered us a disburdening technology that usually entails further separating means from ends. Perhaps it is hollow and shallow. This leaves the heritage travel guide with the aim of curbing participants' deprival disburdenment. Ours is more often an engagement-driven, burdensome technological way of living, where there is something primary and primal that can emerge to warm the spirit beyond warming the body.

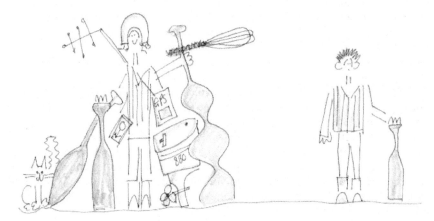

As with the previous section on story and place, technology can also involve making and learning. The making is in creating, for example, a winter camp "home site" for shelter, sustenance, and social enjoyment, or quiet solo time to follow. The making is that singsong / story sharing circle in the evening. The technology learning is found in coming to understand the joy of hands-on engagement inherent in living and travelling in wilderness areas. Connecting means and ends: I must paddle harder in a head wind to make it to the distant campsite. Choosing technology that engages with Nature and advances our primary intimacy with self and place is no minor feat in today's society. Story and place are important components of technology making and learning. Our choice of technological systems (e.g. tarps vs. dome tents, fire vs. stoves, paddle vs. motor) determines stories and our engagement with places.

CONCLUSION

Heritage travel as an orientation to the educational expedition has a cultural emphasis. The intention is for the challenges of understanding an earlier time to help develop an understanding of our own place in time today. These challenges command us to consider how we dwell in the world. What are our stories - the ones we generate from our experiences and the ones we learn to inform our life? What are our places? Where have we made place in our life and what stories about place inform our life? It is my firm belief that understanding a broader meaning of technology through heritage travel can play a crucial role in the ways we form story and identify with place.

These thoughts are philosophical. It is hope they offer a perspective to interpret and challenge conventional ways of seeing the task of education and, specifically, educational expeditions. Whitehead (1972) reminds us that "the aim of philosophic understanding is the aim at piercing the blindness of activity in respect to its transcendent functions" (p. 46). Heritage travel is an educational experience that can entail learning something of the anthropology, history, and literature of peoples in a place in time, as we all dwell in a past, present, and future. There would be a "blindness of the activity" without this emphasis. With a solid attention to the importance of story, place, and understanding technology, there can be a transcendent function that serves as part of our antidote to our modern ways.

John Livingston (1994) noted that "...the antidote to our modern ways of dealing with the world is not technological, not scientific, not even ethical, the modern challenge is metaphysical and ontological – indeed cosmological" (p. vi). The joy and learning for the spirit inherent in the secret of life attests to a powerful learning - a calling to the metaphysical and ontological challenges of our time. The agency, belonging, and competency that ensue impel us to seek reconciliation with the ways in which we dwell in the world. Perhaps educational expeditions can serve as fertile ground to draw out inner world and outer world awareness. As a heritage-based travel guide, I've felt a strong pull to challenge conventional schooling by exploring relations of culture, nature, and community.

Story, place, and technology are not the obvious considerations in planning and implementing outdoor travel. They are, however, central to heritage travel, and are embraced in often subtle and profound ways. "The secret of the lake" as an expression in a student journal following a nine-day camp is a comment that is shrouded in the mystery of story, place, and technological learning on the heritage trail.

IMPLICATIONS FOR PRACTICE

- Expedition providers should examine the role of technology as they equip their trips. The wilderness journey can help students connect means and ends in ways that are uncommon in urban contexts. The primal, burdensome aspects of using older technologies can be an important antecedent to meaningful engagment with nature.

- Leaders should be familiar with the "story" of the landscape through which they are travelling with their students. Furthermore, leaders need to consider pedagogical approaches that will allow students to learn how story enables the expedition "space" to become "place".

- Help make the place come alive! Consider introducing the use of readings and quotes to pepper the travel experience with historical and contemporary cultural context.

- If class assignments accompany a travel experience, consider having students study a local story or interview an area elder. Students then take on the role of storyteller as they share their travel story during time on the trail. They provide a handout of their story for a trip-end booklet that can serve as a local guide.

DISCUSSION QUESTIONS

1. How would an appreciation of the subtle, but important role of story, place, and technology influence you as you guide a new group in the wilds on an educational expedition?

2. Share your own "secret of the lake" stories with others. Consider what common elements exist between stories. What are the cultural implications of this story sharing session and any common elements that might arise?

3. Consider your own practice of travel guiding. What might constitute your own set of warm and green skills?

4. Consider what items of current dominant technology you might do without for a week. What might be lost, but more importantly, what might be gained?

NOTES

[1] In this case, I refer to a nine day field trip with a three-day stay at a base camp and a five-day canoe trip in Lake Country / Canadian Shield. This McMaster University Department of Kinesiology senior course has run continuously since 1982.

REFERENCES

Atwood, M. (1983). *Convocation address at the University of Toronto*. Retrieved September 28, 2009, from http://www.humanity.org/voices/commencements/speeches/index.php?page=atwood_at_toronto

Baldwin, C. (2005). *Storycatcher: Making sense of our lives through the power and practice of story*. Navato, CA: New World Library.

Baker, M. A. (2008). Landfullness in adventure-based programming: Promoting reconnection to the land. In B. Henderson & N. Vikander (Eds.), *Nature first: Outdoor life the frilufisliv way* (pp. 246–256) Toronto, ON: Natural Heritage Books.

Beames, S., & Atencio, M. (2008). Building social capital through outdoor education. *Journal of Adventure Education and Outdoor Learning, 8*(2), 99–112.

Berman, M. (1984). *The re-enactment of the world*. Toronto, ON: Bantam.

Brookes, A. (2002). Gilbert White never came this far south. Naturalist knowledge and the limits of univeralist environmental education. *Canadian Journal of Environmental Education, 7*(2), 73–87.

Carter, K. (1993). The place of story in the study of teaching and teacher education. *Educational Researcher, 22*(2), 5–12.

Chamberlin, C. (Ed.). (1994). *"Don't tell us it can't be done": Alternative classrooms in Canada and abroad*. Toronto, ON: Our Schools/Our Selves Education Foundation.

Cherryholmes, C. (1988). *Power and criticism: Post-structural investigations in education*. New York: Teacher's College Press.

Connelly, F. M., & Clandinin, D. J. (1990). Stories of experience and narrative inquiry. *Educational Researcher, 19*(5), 2–14.

Coupland, D. (1991). *Generation X: Tales for an accelerated culture*. New York: St. Martin's Press.

Cuthbertson, B., Heine, M., & Whitson, D. (1997). Producing meaning through movement: An alternative view of sense of place. *The Trumpeter: Journal of Ecosophy, 14*(2), 72–75.

Duncan, J. D. (1985). *The river why*. New York: Bantam.

Fay, B. (1975). *Social theory and political practice*. London: George Allen & Unwin.

Franklin, U. (1990). *The real world of technology*. Concord, ON: House of Anansi Press.

Grant, G. (1969). *Technology and empire: Perspectives on North America*. Concord, ON: House of Anansi Press.

Henderson, B., Schrader, D., & Roebbelen, E. (2009). Passion is no ordinary word. *Pathways: The Ontario Journal of Outdoor Education, 21*(3), 5–11.

Henderson, B. (2001). Skills and whys: Perceptions of people/native guiding. *The Journal of Outward Bound Canada Education, 7*(3), 12–18.

Jensen, D. (2004). *Walking on water: Reading, writing and revolution.* White River Junction, VT: Chelsea Green.

Livingston, J. (1994). *Rogue primate: An exploration of human domestication.* Toronto, ON: Key Porter.

Meeker, J. W. (1974). *The comedy of survival: Studies in literary ecology.* New York: Simon & Schuster.

Neill, J. T. (2008). *Enhancing life effectiveness: The impacts of outdoor education programs.* Unpublished doctoral dissertation, University of Western Sydney, Australia. Retrieved March 29, 2009, from http://wilderdom.com/phd2/Neill2008EnhancingLifeEffectivenessTheImpactsOfOutdoorEducation Programs.pdf

Park, S. (2007). Enacting a curriculum of life: Mindfulness and complexity thinking in the classroom. *Paideusis, 16*(30), 45–55.

Said, E. (1993). *Culture and imperialism.* New York: Alfred A. Knopf.

Stevens, W. (1942). *The necessary angle: Essays on reality and the imagination.* New York: Vintage Books.

Strong, D. (1995). *Crazy mountains: Learning from wilderness to weigh technology.* Albany, NY: SUNY Press.

Swimme, B., & Berry, T. (1992). *The universe story.* New York: Harper Collins.

Tuan, Y. F. (1977). *Space and place: The perspective of experience.* Minneapolis, MN: University of Minnesota Press.

Whitehead, A. N. ([1933] 1967). *Adventures of ideas.* New York: The Free Press.

Whitehead, A. N. (1972). *Whitehead's philosophy: Selected essays 1935–1970.* Lincoln: University of Nebraska Press.

Bob Henderson
McMaster University

JOHN CROSBIE

9. EXPEDITIONS FOR PEOPLE WITH DISABILITIES

Including people with disabilities in an expedition will inevitably affect some aspect of the experience and has the potential to change it completely. Whether this impact is viewed as positive or negative will depend on the expedition in question and the attitude of the organisers, leaders and other participants.

The fact that an expedition includes disabled people may be regarded as a benefit in itself as this will address a number of societal, moral and legal obligations (Americans with Disabilities Act, 1990; Disability Discrimination Act, 1995). In addition, Anderson, Schleien, McAvoy, Lais, & Seligman (1997) state "it is widely accepted that the integration of people with disabilities in adventure education programmes has benefits for ... people without disabilities" (p. 215). These benefits may include a decrease in stereotyping (Ewert, 1989) and a change in attitude and interpersonal relationships between non-disabled and disabled people (Edwards & Smith, 1989; McAvoy, Schatz, Stutz, Schleien, & Lais, 1989; Sable, 1995).

The potential benefits of the expedition for the participants with disabilities will be the same as those for the other expedition members. However, the different life experiences and the different expectations for the expedition often create a very different starting point for the experience (Carpenter, 1994; McAvoy & Lais, 1999), which can result in additional outcomes that are not available to non-disabled participants. These outcomes may include: increased social adjustment, increased self-understanding, increased awareness of their own capabilities and an increased ability to accomplish difficult or challenging tasks in daily life (McAvoy, Holman, Goldenberg, & Klenosky, 2006).

As with any expedition, some outcomes will naturally occur through participation alone, while other outcomes will require careful planning, programming and appropriate processes to deliver the desired results. For people with disabilities, part of the process may be in the approach to their involvement in the expedition.

APPROACHES

There are many reasons for expeditions to include people with disabilities and many models of how this may be achieved. It would be wonderful if the reason for inclusion is that the participants who happen to have a disability are regarded as equally valued members of society and that the design of the expedition from its outset considers the needs of all potential participants. However, this idealistic situation is seldom, if ever, the case. People with a disability are a non-homogenous minority with diverse needs that have rarely been taken into account in the design of service provision and equipment in contemporary society. Expeditions are likely

S. K. Beames (ed.), Understanding Educational Expeditions, 91–101.
© 2010 Sense Publishers. All rights reserved.

to be challenging by their nature, but once the potential range of disabilities has been accommodated, they may fail to meet the needs of any of the participants. A more pragmatic approach is to take the expedition and its purpose as the starting point and consider how it may be adapted to include people with disabilities. Alternatively, one could start with the people for whom the expedition is intended, and then design an expedition which will meet their needs and enable their full participation. These two approaches may be described as "geographically centred" or "people centred" expeditions (Crosbie, 1997) and are no different to any other expedition. An expedition for the first ascent of a mountain will identify the skills mix needed in the team members. If, for example, a medic is required but cannot be found with the requisite climbing skills, then techniques or compromises will have to be developed to enable their safe involvement. Similarly, a school expedition would not take on a trip that is outside the capabilities of its participants.

The main aim of an expedition should not be changed just because it is intended to include people with disabilities. In the same way, the main purpose for involvement in an expedition should be the same for both the disabled and non-disabled participants. However, there are some aims that may form part of the overt or hidden agenda for either the organisers or the participants. Crosbie (1997) identified a number of reasons why an expedition might wish to involve people with disabilities.

Normalisation. If provided with the opportunity to participate in activities regarded as "normal" by non-disabled people, people with disabilities may be more able to discuss their experiences with those from a broader section of society. This opportunity for socialising between non-disabled and disabled peers often leads to a greater understanding of each others' needs and viewpoints, thus breaking down some of the perceived barriers that the different life experiences can create. Hence, providing the pathway for continued involvement in the activity with non-disabled groups or sports organisations must be a natural extension of this process.

Life-skills Training. Participation in the expedition may be used as motivator to help develop skills in "activities for daily living". These activities may be simple life skills such as dressing, being on time for events, or making a cup of tea, to higher level skills such as time management and organisational ability.

Rehabilitation. The above life-skills training could be developed to enable an individual to better manage issues related to their disability (e.g. bowel / bladder management or being appropriately prepared for specific events despite their disability). Overcoming disability issues may increase independence, employability and the ability to maintain relationships - all of which are regarded as goals of rehabilitation. By dealing with the issues relating to the expedition, an approach to overcoming challenges that can be transferred to other situations may be acquired.

Demonstration of Ability. An opportunity for proving a point to themselves, family and peers, or wider society may alter perceptions of what is possible for someone with a disability to achieve. If the demonstration of ability relates to a phenomenal task or one perceived as impossible, then less or not so challenging tasks of everyday living may be regarded as even more achievable.

Freedom from Disabling Elements / Attitudes in Society. Undertaking activities that have been adapted to remove the barriers associated with impairment eliminates the emphasis on the individual's disability. Similarly, through participation in an expedition exclusively for people with disabilities, the participants are relieved from being the focus of attention and can be allowed to complete tasks independently within their own time-frame. This opportunity may provide a sense of freedom seldom experienced in many disabled people's lives.

Fund-raising. The inclusion of people with disabilities is frequently used to raise money which enables the expedition to proceed, or to raise money (as in a sponsored event) for other projects. In my experience of working with fund-giving organisations in the UK, the introduction of the DDA has reduced the number of donations supporting people with disabilities participating in expeditions, as fund-givers are reluctant to subsidise activities that organisations that have a legal obligation to provide.

Clearly establishing the aims of the expedition and the reasons for inclusion should, generally, guide organisers to the most appropriate model for participation. If this does not occur, then the reasons for inclusion will need to be carefully thought through in order to ensure that those the expedition intends to embrace are not disenfranchised by the adopted model (Crosbie, 1997).

MODELS FOR PARTICIPATION

Crosbie (1997) identified the following models of involving people with disabilities in expeditions. It is intended to provide a synopsis of approaches that could be adopted. The terms used do not enjoy universal understanding in their meaning. However, they are those in common use and are supported by definitions from the (Oxford Concise Dictionary, 2003).

Inclusion

"*Include* - Comprise or contain as part of a whole"

As in the example given earlier, inclusive expeditions are designed from the outset to include people with disabilities. Participants' specific needs have been considered in order for each person to be fully functioning member within the whole programme. In a school, this is where a disabled pupil's learning takes place in a class alongside their non-disabled peers.

Integration

"*Integrate* - combine or be combined to form a whole"

In outdoor settings, "integration" often involves a group of people with disabilities sharing some of the facilities with non-disabled people (e.g. domestic or outdoor resources), but undertaking a different programme that is more suitable for their needs. In a school setting, this would involve having a "special needs" class within the school.

Parallel Activity

"*Parallel* – side by side but having ... distance between them."

This will involve an appropriate alternative activity when the participants cannot be catered for within the planned mainstream activity. In the outdoors, this may involve a low level or surfaced walk rather than a mountain walk. In a school, this may involve the pupils in an "inclusive" class undertaking separate physical education lessons, as they cannot participate in the sports offered to non-disabled pupils.

Specialist Provision

"*Specialist* – concentrating on a particular subject or activity. A person highly skilled in a specific field"

An alternative viewpoint may regard this specialist provision as segregation or exclusion. However, the definition does indicate a quality of the provision that might be missing in some of the more inclusive offerings, which, through a lack of resources, may have to adopt a "make do" attitude. Specialisation may be contrary to the ideals of social justice, but it remains the preferred option for many disabled people. Indeed, research indicates that only those with a congenital physical disability have a preference for integrated recreation activities (Zoerink, 1989). A specialist provider may still allow participation by non-disabled people, if both the quality offered by the specialist provider and inclusion are required. However, such an arrangement may not be acceptable to some disabled people, non-disabled people, or the specialist provider.

Tokenist

"*Tokenist* – making only perfunctory or symbolic effort ... recruiting a small number of people from under-represented groups in order to give the appearance of equality"

Although the tokenist approach may be viewed as disreputable, it still provides opportunities for some disabled people (and even some non-disabled people) to participate in an expedition that otherwise could not have gone ahead due to lack of support from the authorities or funders.

It is very easy to become judgemental as to the right and wrong approaches for people with disabilities to be involved in expeditions. However, it is probably much safer to weigh the merits of each model in the circumstances in which one finds oneself, adopt the most appropriate approach for the expedition's specific participants, and be prepared to justify the reasons for the chosen approach.

PRACTICALITIES

Adjustments

Programme adjustments will probably be required to accommodate participants with disabilities, but the adjustments needed will depend on the individuals involved, the nature of their disabilities and the intended expedition.

Some combinations of individuals, their disabilities and expeditions will require few or no adjustments whatsoever. Where adjustments are needed, the factors that can increase the ability of someone to participate include: the choice of terrain (surface, gradient, total climbing required), mode of transport (e.g. canoe instead of kayak, catamaran instead of mono-hull sailing boat, horse instead of foot, skidoo instead of ski), distance to be travelled, length of day, and frequency and number of stops. The latter could be combined with skills training, field work or another purpose integral to the expedition, rather than focusing on an individual's ability.

If the necessary adjustments are so great that the nature of the expedition is substantially affected, then this may be justification in UK law (DDA, 1995) for discriminating against the person with a disability. Under these circumstances, the individual may be lawfully excluded from certain aspects of the expedition or possibly the expedition altogether. Organisers should only consider this as the last resort, having first exhausted all of the alternatives that do not substantially alter the nature of the expedition.

Adaptive Equipment

Adaptive equipment may be required to enable some participants to fully engage or even participate at all in the activities related to the expedition. Although it is helpful to be aware of the range of adaptive equipment available, it is more important to discuss with the individual what their actual needs are and address those needs, rather than make assumptions about their needs or the equipment required. Additional equipment may create significant logistical issues, alter the expedition's nature, or even jeopardise its viability. The participants with disabilities may have to make compromises to their ideal solution and accept a certain level of tolerance with makeshift alternatives, particularly with respect to domestic needs. However, this is the same for other participants - all of whom must sacrifice some of their "home comforts". Participants with disabilities are likely to have limited experience of expeditions, but will certainly possess an intricate knowledge of their own functionality. This may result in certain items of equipment being regarded as an essential to the individual, but being viewed as a luxury by the organisers. The negotiations needed to reach the correct balance require empathy, tact and diplomacy.

Risk

The perceived increase in physical risk when involving people with disabilities in expeditions is a major barrier to their involvement within our risk-averse society. All expeditions have an element of risk inherent within them but it is only when particular individuals with their specific disabilities combine with certain environments that there is any increased risk, and this in turn may impact on the expedition.

The fact that a person has a disability should not prevent them from participating in an expedition *per se*. However, an individual's physical or cognitive competence to perform at the level required by the circumstances may affect the safety of that individual, the group, or to the ability of the expedition to progress in order for it to fulfil its objective. Only then will action need to be taken to control the risks. This control may be achieved by a change in equipment (e.g. mode of transport, type of accommodation, adaptive aids) or a change of environment (e.g. route choice, location, availability of support). Note that adjustments as above are appropriate for controlling risk on any expedition, whether or not it includes people with disabilities. Finally, if the risk cannot be controlled to an acceptable level, exclusion of the individual will need to be a consideration. The latter must, to a certain extent, be regarded as a failure on behalf of the expedition organiser / leader not to have found an acceptable alternative.

It can be seen that the risks involved with including people with disabilities on expeditions should be treated in the same way as other risk management issues in the outdoors. Once the risk has been identified and assessed, controlling measures are put in place or alternative plans must be made. The difficulty for many outdoor practitioners is that although they have the expertise to control risks involved with an "outdoor hazard", they do not always have the knowledge of how to moderate the risks associated with a "disability hazard". Thus, the hazard is observed but the solutions required to moderate the risk to an acceptable level are not taken into account. Assistance in finding solutions may be achieved by involving the individual or group of people with disabilities, obtaining the advice of a technical expert (disability, medical, or outdoor), and usually some creative thinking.

Attitude

A positive attitude by all participants towards those with a disability is essential to the success of an inclusive expedition. Any notion that the people with disabilities are "to blame" for any compromise in the programme must be addressed at an early stage. If a compromise has been made, all participants should have been party to the negotiation, rather than the outcome being forced upon them, thus reducing the chance for negative attitudes to develop. Similarly, care should be taken to ensure that people with disabilities are not made to feel they are the "problems" for the expedition group to overcome, as this will generate a feeling of dependency with resultant low self-worth for those people (Dixon & Caradoc-Davies, 2005;

Gignac, Cott, & Badley, 2000). Some believe that receiving assistance in these circumstances is positive as it results in a degree of "interdependence" between disabled and non-disabled people (Corbett, 1997; Goodwin, Peco, & Ginther, 1990). However, I would argue that these writers use the terms "independence" and "interdependence" differently than in everyday use, and that the disabled participant's reliance on the non-disabled person is "dependence" as the non-disabled person is not reliant on the disabled participant (although they may contribute in many ways). It may be valuable to identify those tasks or components of a task that the participants with disabilities can fully perform, and ensure that they have the opportunity to function at their maximum potential in this specific area. This way they can be seen as contributors to the expedition as a whole and cannot be viewed as "excess baggage". Steps should be taken to ensure that some chore is not kept exclusively for those with a disability, such as cook or pot wash duties (Lais, 1987).

Personal Care

Personal care issues may be considered as falling into one of three distinct areas. These are the physical environment (terrain, surfaces, accessibility, availability of facilities), requirements which would enable an individual to complete the task themselves (time, specialist equipment, medication, accessible toilet availability), and any outside assistance that may be needed (mobility assistance, organisational assistance, behaviour management) (Crosbie, 1996). If the assistance involves personal care, intrusive medical practices or specific "trained" skills, it is likely that a personal assistant or specialist care staff will be required.

Moving and handling (lifting) people is an area of contention within the "care communities." The availability of mechanical hoists in many care situations has resulted in minimising the amount of manual handling undertaken by support staff, and many organisations have adopted blanket "no lifting" policies. Unfortunately, although this may be best practice in the "built" care environment, it is not always "reasonably practical" (Health and Safety Executive, 2004) in an outdoor setting or on expeditions (Crosbie, 2007) and is contrary to UK case law[1]. However, safe techniques for moving people must be employed and it is essential to plan any "transfers" that will be required and ensure the availability of the equipment needed to undertake them.

A personal care plan (PCP) is a tool which may be used to record the help, equipment or techniques needed by a specific individual. It can include transfer or lifting techniques to be used in given circumstances. This plan may be used to address the UK Heath & Safety Executive requirements of a recorded risk assessment for the involvement of an individual on the expedition. Details on the plan could be restricted to medical or domestic situations, alternatively, or can be extended to activity situations as well.

As an example, let us consider a person participating in a canoe expedition who has a head injury (with resultant hemiplegia and epilepsy), who also uses a wheel chair to assist mobility.

CROSBIE

DOMESTIC PLAN

Mobility around campsites
- A variety of differing surfaces will be encountered. A chair with large rear wheels will maximise mobility and reduce assistance / manual handling issues.
- Where surfaces are smooth and hard (e.g. surfaced paths) independent mobility is possible. On rougher ground (e.g. short grass), an assistant / pusher will be needed. On very rough ground (sand, shingle, mud, or steep inclines), haul lines attached to the chair and a team of helpers will be required.

Transfer needs
- Can transfer chair to chair without assistance but requires some (non-professional) help in chair to floor transfers.

Accommodation needs
- High roofed tent to allow wheelchair access and assistance with bed to chair transfer. Air-bed to minimise risk of pressure sores. Fully zipped sleeping bag to ease access.

Eating / dressing
- Assistance needed with cutting food. Adaptive plate and cutlery required. Can dress independently but time needed. Assistance required with helmet & Personal Floatation Device.

Toilet / shower
- Adapted folding chair will enable latrine and shower use.

Equipment needs
- Folding chair, cutlery, crockery, wheel chair, walking stick, air-bed, extra large waterproof trousers, open fronted PFD, supportive seating in canoe.

ACTIVITY PLAN

Transfer to canoe
- Rough terrain, vertical height differences, and canoe being unstable means that assistance will be required in transferring to and from the canoe. Patient handling sling and four participants trained to assist will enable transfer to take place under all anticipated circumstances.

Assistance on water
- Standard paddle can be used. May lose balance in waves, thus seating with lateral support required in canoe. With an experienced rear paddler, this will maintain stability up to grade 2 water, beyond which capsize is probable. A canoe-raft (duckie), with seating available on the bottom of the craft, is to be used above grade 2 water.

Rescue
- Confident in water but limited swimming ability. Avoiding a capsize is preferable to recovering from one. So, if there is any doubt about ability to negotiate any rapid in which a "swim" would be hazardous, then the "duckie" is to be used. A capsize will be recovered on the bank only.

Emergencies
- A continuous epileptic seizure (beyond 20 minutes) will require intrusive medical intervention. Hence an assistant is required who is trained in intrusive medical techniques. They are to be within the same group at all times. No foreseeable requirement for evacuation, but if needed, this will be as for any other member of the party.

98

PITFALLS & BARRIERS

The main pitfalls in planning an expedition for people with disabilities are: a lack of clarity of purpose for their inclusion; making assumptions about the needs of the disabled participants; and being too purist in the expedition's chosen approach, and consequently failing to make sufficient compromises to enable their participation. Any single one of the above, or combination of them, may create an attitudinal barrier to participation which can be greater than any of the many other barriers faced by disabled people.

Of these other barriers, the most significant are likely to be the confidence and experience of the leaders in running an expedition of this nature. This will include their knowledge of appropriate adaptive equipment, as well as their skills in delivering the activity to people with a diverse range of disabilities. The other significant barrier will be the issues related to the logistics and the practicalities of what can be achieved within the constraints of the expedition.

Opening an expedition to people with disabilities is likely to incur an additional cost that is directly attributable to their inclusion. The question of how that extra cost can be borne is inevitable. The expedition may be viewed as having a single cost to be shared by all participants. However, sharing the additional costs may place the expedition financially out of reach of some non-disabled participants who do not require the additional facilities. An alternative would be for those who benefit from the additional facilities to fund them. This places an increased burden on the few who already have other barriers to participation and have additional costs of living because of their disability. This group is likely to have a lower income as disabled people have a higher rate of unemployment. So, to ask the disabled participants to finance the additional costs may exclude them from participation. Accessing "third party" funding would solve this dilemma, but potentially places a stigma on the disabled participants as they become "charity cases" and, as mentioned above, fund-givers are becoming less likely to support an event when the organisers have a legal obligation to provide the service. If the onus of responsibility lies with the organisers, they may have to divert funds from sources which could have been used for other purposes. The organiser may view the financial burden of opening access to disabled people as "unreasonable", thus negating the requirement for them to make the adjustments and so justifying the exclusion of disabled people from the expedition!

CONCLUSION

The inclusion of people with disabilities on an expedition may enhance the objectives of the expedition, while addressing moral and legal obligations. Although there are a number of practical and logistical issues that need to be addressed, these are seldom insurmountable. With the right attitude, a certain amount of compromise, and plenty of creative thinking, many expeditions could be opened up to a range of people with disabilities.

IMPLICATIONS FOR PRACTICE

- Know why you are organising an expedition that is integrated or only for people with disabilities.

- Be aware of the adaptive equipment available, its use, and its appropriateness for your expedition.

- Consult with the participants with disabilities, or, where appropriate, their care assistants, as to their needs, wants, and likes. Ensure you are aware which fall into which category, as well as their compatibility with the ethos of the expedition.

- Find a compromise without jeopardising the expedition, while remembering that you have a moral or legal obligation to make "reasonable adjustments".

- It is better to do more to accommodate someone with a disability than may be required by the legislation. However, if you have to discriminate against someone because of their disability, ensure that you are familiar with the legislation pertaining to your circumstances.

DISCUSSION QUESTIONS

Consider a recent expedition in which you have participated.

1. What range of disabilities could have been included in the expedition without any adaptations?

2. What range of disabilities could have been included with adaptations, and what would be the necessary adaptations?

3. What are the safety implications of including a person with one of the identified disabilities on the expedition and how would you address these?

Draw up a Personal Care Plan for the person in the above example.

NOTES

[1] In 2003 the judge in the case between R v East Sussex County Council, concluded that a lifting policy is "most unlikely to be lawful which, either on its face or in its application, imposes a blanket ban on manual lifting". (Disability Rights Commission, 2003)

REFERENCES

ADA. (1990). *Americans with disabilities act*. Washington, DC: US Dept of Justice.
Anderson, L., Schleien, S., McAvoy, L., Lais, G., & Seligman, D. (1997). Creating positive change through an integrated outdoor adventure program. *Therapeutic Recreation Journal, 31*(4), 214–229.
Carpenter, C. (1994). The experience of spinal cord injury: The individual's perspective-implications for rehabilitation practice. *Physical Therapy, 74*(7), 614–629.

Corbett, J. (1997). Independent, proud and special: Celebrating our differences. In L. Barton & M. Oliver (Eds.), *Disability studies: Past present and future* (pp. 90–98). Leeds, UK: The Disability Press.

Crosbie, J. (1996). *Disability awareness training course notes.* Keswick, UK: Calvert Trust.

Crosbie, J. (1997). *Philosophy.* In G. Smedley (Ed.), *Canoe expeditions for people with disabilities* (pp. 9–12). Nottingham, UK: British Canoe Union.

Crosbie, J. (Writer). (2007). Moving and handling people in the outdoors [DVD]. In *Escape productions.* Keswick, UK: Calvert Trust.

DDA. (1995). *Disability discrimination act.* London: Stationery Office.

Disability Rights Commission. (2003). *R v East Sussex County Council Ex parte A, B, X and Y High Court.* Retrieved from DRC/ the_law/drc_legal cases/interventions

Dixon, G. S., & Caradoc-Davies, T. H. (2005). The work of rehabilitation. *Disability & Rehabilitation, 27,* 643–648.

Edwards, D., & Smith, R. (1989). Social interaction in an integrated day camp setting. *Therapeutic Recreation Journal, 23*(3), 71–78.

Ewert, A. (1989). *Outdoor adventure pursuits: Foundations, models, and theories.* Columbus, OH: Publishing Horizons.

Gignac, M., Cott, C., & Badley, E. (2000). Adaptation to chronic illness and disability and its relationship to perceptions of independence and dependence. *Journals of Gerontology, 55B*(6), P362–P372.

Goodwin, D., Peco, J., & Ginther, N. (1990). Hiking excursions for persons with disabilities: Experiences of interdependence. *Therapeutic Recreation Journal, 43*(1), 43–55.

Health and Safety Executive. (2004). *Manual handling. Manual handling operations regulations 1992 (as amended 2002).* London: HMSO.

Lais, G. (1987). Towards fullest participation—suggested leadership techniques for integrated adventure programming. In G. M. Robb (Ed.), *The Bradford Papers Annual* (Vol. 2). Bloomington, IN: Parks and Recreation Association.

McAvoy, L., Holman, T., Goldenberg, M., & Klenosky, D. (2006). Wilderness and persons with disabilities: Transferring the benefits to everyday life. *International Journal of Wilderness, 12*(2), 23–31, 35.

McAvoy, L., & Lais, G. (1999). Programs that include persons with disabilities. In J. Miles & S. Priest (Eds.), *Adventure programming* (pp. 403–414). State College: Venture.

McAvoy, L., Schatz, E. C., Stutz, M. E., Schleien, S. J., & Lais, G. (1989). Integrated wilderness adventure: Effects on personal lifestyle traits of persons with and without disabilities. *Therapeutic Recreation Journal, 23*(3), 51–64.

Oxford Concise Dictionary. (2003). Oxford, UK: Oxford University Press.

Sable, J. R. (1995). Efficacy of physical integration, disability awareness, and adventure programming on adolescents' acceptance of individuals with disabilities. *Therapeutic Recreation Journal, 29*(3), 206–217.

Zoerink, D. (1989). Activity choices: Exploring perceptions of persons with physical disabilities. *Therapeutic Recreation Journal, 23*(1), 17–23.

John Crosbie
University of Edinburgh / Calvert Trust

ANDREA NIGHTINGALE

10. ETHICS FOR EXPEDITIONS

Expeditions can offer a rich variety of learning experiences. This chapter addresses a critical, yet often over-looked component of learning on expeditions: ethics. Sometimes the greatest learning that can take place is through the challenges of "doing no harm" in the context of your travels (Hay & Foley, 1998). In working with scientific expeditions, I have found that most expeditions neglect to take seriously the range of ethical issues that can arise, despite many of these very issues being what causes an expedition to succeed or fail. I will first explain a bit about what I mean by "ethics" and why it merits thoughtful consideration. I will then work through a few examples from the field that may help you to plan your own consideration of ethics.

WHAT IS ETHICS?

Ethics is the study of ethical theory and conduct. Within academia, people in philosophy, geography, anthropology, animal biology, and health have all contributed to understanding ethics in research and expeditions - either conceptually or pragmatically (Hay & Foley, 1998; Light & Smith, 1997; Proctor, 1998; Robson, 2002; Rose, 1993; Sayer & Storper, 1997; Smith, 1997). Fundamentally, all ethical theories are concerned with right and wrong, good and bad. Although most have focused on human conduct, animal ethics and environmental ethics consider the non-human as well (Light & Smith, 1997). In expeditions, frequently both are highly relevant - even if you are studying small mammals or rainforest plants. This chapter offers some background and guidance on how to identify the ethical issues relevant to your work.

Most ethical theorists make a distinction between descriptive and normative ethics (Hay & Foley, 1998; Smith, 1997). Descriptive ethics describes the moral beliefs and behaviours found in different human communities. Here the focus is on what kinds of moral beliefs different cultures adhere to and how they may differ. Normative ethics, on the other hand, is concerned with developing and applying ethical theories to moral problems. There are a number of sub-theories within normative ethics that seek to explain how moral beliefs are universal. While most people reject this stance, many have suggested there are sets of principles that apply across time, space, and culture. It is this latter interpretation that drives the ethical standards discussed below. Without accepting that some moral principles can be universal, it is impossible to develop ethical guidelines.

When we look to apply ethics to decision making, there are three broad theories that have been put forward over centuries of philosophical enquiry. On expedition, you may find that you draw on one or the other of these. The first, utilitarianism,

S. K. Beames (ed.), Understanding Educational Expeditions, 103–112.
© 2010 Sense Publishers. All rights reserved.

suggests that moral decisions should be based on promoting the greatest good for the greatest number - even if it means taking an action that might cause harm for some (Mill, Bentham, & Ryan, 1987). This is the kind of reasoning that is used to justify triage practices after a car accident, for example. Patients who have only minor injuries, or who are the most severely injured but would monopolise the rescue team, are left until last, while people who can be quickly stabilised are helped first. The second moral decision-making paradigm is that put forward by Kant, which states that doing one's duty or following a moral principle regardless of the consequences is the most appropriate guideline for ethical conduct (Baron, Pettit, & Slote, 1997). Here, you may come to the same triage principles, but would also be possible to leave more people to suffer while you help the person identified in your paradigm as the most important one to help. On expeditions, this kind of *de-ontological* moral reasoning can be very challenging to follow, as you may find that your moral principles do not neatly translate into the context within which you are working. This will be discussed further when thinking about interpreting ethical guidelines. The third theory is one based on an ethic of care (Held, 2006). Here, moral decisions are guided by care for other people or non-humans, with a particular understanding of dependent (or caring) relations between people in particular circumstances. An ethics of care departs from classical theories of ethics in that it emphasises the relationships and emotions involved in a given situation. Universal, abstract principles of "right" and "wrong" are replaced with an understanding of the need to situate, interpret and evaluate each context from a "caring ethical" standpoint. As such, an ethics of care can provide important resources when faced with unfamiliar, challenging and sometimes dangerous situations. With these ethical paradigms in mind, I now want to work through why ethics are important in expeditions and how to develop good working frameworks for your expedition.

WHY ATTEND TO ETHICS?

There are two important reasons for attending to ethics on expeditions: moral reasons and legal protection. As we have seen, ethics is concerned with avoiding harm to other people or species. However, how we interpret what this means depends on the ethical paradigm adopted. From a moral perspective, then, you may believe that your expedition has no need to worry about doing harm, but it is quite possible that you could cause people or other species physical or psychological distress - even if they are not directly involved in the work. Further, many expedition teams assume that because they themselves are excited about their work, the people they encounter will also be similarly excited. Yet, clearly this is not necessarily the case, and from a moral perspective, it is crucial that you respect the privacy of others and the right of people you encounter to avoid involvement in your project.

Legally, it is relatively simple. Increasingly, a condition of receiving funding for an expedition is ethics clearance. Failure to attend to ethics could leave the expedition vulnerable to legal action due to ethical violations. The laws have been changing, so it is important to stay up to date with your obligations and ensure that you meet the minimum requirements. Most of your legal obligations can be fulfilled by following a set of ethical guidelines or codes. The next section takes a look at some of these codes.

Ethical codes

There are a number of sources for information on ethical codes and guidelines. The websites of major scientific funding bodies (e.g. ESRC, NERC) as well as organisations like the British Sociological Association or the Royal Geographical Society have ethical guidelines published on their websites. These are good sources for codes relating to both physical science and social science research. These guidelines are similar and most are founded on the principles of "do no harm". Therefore, they emphasise issues like:

The protection of research participants and people you encounter on your expedition by:
– Obtaining voluntary consent
– Respecting confidentiality
– Ensuring the research does not secondarily cause harm (e.g. by revealing sensitive information to an outside source)

The protection of endangered species or areas that are ecologically sensitive by:
– Not removing samples of plants, animals or rocks from study areas
– Ensuring that travel and camping arrangements are "minimum impact" (http://www.lnt.org/training/educationaltraining.php)

Following ethical guidelines can help your expedition meet legal requirements and will give you an overview of issues to which you need to attend. Legal requirements and guidelines can provide a framework for thinking through ethics, but they operate from a set of standards that cannot fully anticipate all ethical dilemmas, and consequently, cannot guide you in every ethical issue encountered in the field. Rather, your expedition is likely to come across situations where the ethical issues are not clear cut, and which require you to make difficult choices. In order to prepare yourself for such choices, it is important to consider the interpretation of ethical guidelines.

INTERPRETING ETHICS

Keeping your expedition free of legal liability is undoubtedly easier than attending to the myriad of moral issues that your expedition can elicit. When we operate from a moral paradigm, ethical issues become more complex and we find that our codes of conduct are often woefully inadequate. This is because it is not possible to develop a code that will always lead to the right behaviour. Rather, you need to use your judgement in the field to interpret ethical codes when you are faced with complex situations. While not causing harm is a good guiding principle, it is often insufficient. Most importantly, what "doing no harm" means is not necessarily universally understood (or obvious) in different situations. While principles like "not killing" are fairly straight-forward, issues surrounding photography, travel and work in areas that may be sacred, or contact with populations (whether animal, plant or human) that have not been exposed to the "outside" in recent times, become much more complex. You will have to decide if the goals of the expedition and its potential impact are compatible or if one is more important than the other. Learning the moral codes of the place you are visiting and having a basic understanding of the host culture will help you to interpret ethical codes in your field area. Thinking through how this background information might inform ethical choices in the field will also prepare you for making those judgements in situations that may be more pressured and require a rapid response.

From a moral perspective, then, you may adopt a more detailed or strict understanding of the ethical issues surrounding your expedition than the minimum standard required for legal clearance. Some of these issues we can group under the headings of respect, honesty, and conflicts of interest.

Respect

It is relatively easy to say "respect the people you encounter" but what exactly does this mean? Is it respectful if your main objective in talking to people is to extract information? Do you have an obligation to give something back? Is it ethical to covertly tape record an interview? Often on expeditions, you find that issues of respect and dignity may not be as easy to follow they sound on paper. Think through how the following may complicate your ethical considerations:

– The need to treat human or non-human subjects as "ends in themselves" rather than as a means to your ends
– Participants should give free and informed consent (without manipulation, coercion or undue influence)

- Respect the privacy and confidentiality of participants
- Data Protection Act. How should you store and make available your results?
- Respect for vulnerable persons
- Respect for difference: cultural, religious, gender, sexual

The first point, treating subjects as "ends in themselves", can shift significantly your approach to the expedition. Often on an expedition, goals may seem to be the most important consideration and the needs, wishes, and impact on the people and non-humans you encounter can be forgotten. If you adopt a perspective that places the dignity of the other beings you encounter in the centre of your considerations (e.g. an ethics of care (Held, 2006)), you may choose to conduct aspects of your expedition in a different manner. Yet, what this means in practice may not be as easy to implement as it sounds. Take, for example, the final bullet point: respect for difference. While you may believe you are respecting difference, it is impossible to fully understand another culture and unless you have years of experience; you will undoubtedly transgress culturally appropriate behaviour at some point. Rather than seeking for complete information, it is important to keep in mind that you do not fully understand the context you are entering. This puts the onus on you to pay more attention to when you may need to approach a situation with caution, ask questions, take corrective action, apologise, or shift your strategies as you become more aware of the context. The important point to remember is that the expedition should be designed to maximize the extent to which you can understand the overall cultural context (even if this seems irrelevant to your aims), and that you need to continually evaluate, ask questions, act with humility, and be prepared to change tactics.

A good example of an expedition that caused unintended physical and psychological harm by failing to respect local cultural and religious traditions occurred in Humla district, north-western Nepal, many years ago. An international team of climbers set out to climb an 8000 meter peak in the district and, upon reaching the top, they planted a flag. Pleased that they achieved their goal, the expedition left the area believing that they had caused no harm. That year the crops failed in Humla and local people began to suspect that it was caused by the flag. The mountain climbed by the expedition was sacred and the indigenous people believed a god lived upon it. They therefore worried that the flag offended the god and, subsequently, several local people set out to climb the mountain and remove the flag. Unsurprisingly, in the absence of mountaineering experience and proper equipment, they were not successful and those who tried, died.

What are the ethical issues that arise in this example? First, the expedition clearly caused psychological distress and worse, people died as a result. Did the expedition have an obligation to anticipate this outcome? From a legal perspective, at the moment the law is vague. The expedition team did not encourage people to try to climb the mountain and therefore they were not legally liable for this unintended tragedy. But from a moral perspective, the visitors are arguably culpable. As discussed above, ethical obligations extend to understanding the cultural context. If the expedition had done adequate background research on the area, they may have learned that the mountain was sacred and could have attempted to find out if certain actions would be considered offensive. In this case, such background research may well have led to the conclusion that planting a flag was, indeed, perfectly acceptable. In Nepal, one way to honour gods is to hang prayer flags (a Tibetan tradition) or to put colourful strips of cloth on a shrine. From this perspective, the visitors might have concluded that planting a flag would be fine. However, a better approach would have been to decide with the locals whether a flag was acceptable. If local people sanctioned the planting of the flag, they would have been much less likely to blame crop failure on it. In this case, dialog with local people helps to respect the dignity and wishes of the people encountered. Most importantly, by giving the locals a voice in what the team did on the mountain, the expedition not only fulfils their ethical obligations from a moral standpoint, but they are also less likely to have legal issues arise. In other words, it would be easier for the expedition to demonstrate that they met their legal ethical requirements had they engaged local people in a discussion of their planned actions prior to starting the expedition.

Honesty and Accountability

Ethical codes dictate that you are honest during an expedition. But again, what does this mean? You may have a write up of the expedition and its goals to distribute to people, but if it is written in a language or style that local people cannot understand, is that an honest representation of the work? What if an official-looking document is threatening or can be used as an excuse by locals to push their own agenda? Think about the following elements of honesty:

– Honesty in your own actions and in your responses to the actions of others
– Honesty in how you represent your expedition and its goals
– Acknowledgement of others' contributions to your expedition, including the importance of local facilitators in making your expedition successful
– Keeping your expedition consistent with the terms of your original agreement with your funding bodies
– Appropriate use of finances

Honesty is situated. This means that it is most appropriate to convey what your expedition is about in terms that people will understand. For example, when I worked in north-western Nepal I was frequently asked if I had a boyfriend back home. Nepalis knew that westerners had boyfriends - something which was totally taboo in their culture at that time (this has changed recently). So, if I had simply answered "yes", I would create an image of myself that was not accurate. Instead, I answered that question depending on the person asking. If it was someone who knew me relatively well and was clearly curious about my culture, I answered "yes" and went on to explain how boyfriends are perceived in our culture in contrast to their own. I tried to place it in context so that they could understand the moral implications for me. If it was a man who was effectively trying to find out if I was available—indeed, many of them saw having a boyfriend as a sort of prostitution—I answered an indignant "no". Their reasons for asking were not innocent and to have answered "honestly" would have been a dishonest portrayal of the kind of person I am morally within my own context. As we can see in this example, it is not always a case of simply stating who you are or the goals of your expedition to everyone you meet. You may need to understand something about their world view and try to understand how your actions would be perceived within that.

Another important component of honesty is to give appropriate credit to those who facilitate your expedition. To claim that you pioneered a first ascent of a mountain when you had local guides who supported and guided the expedition until the penultimate ascent, would be dishonest. Most expeditions and remote fieldwork are impossible without the support and consent of local people, and sufficiently acknowledging them in your results is important for giving an accurate portrayal of your outcomes. You should not see this as detracting from your accomplishments. If you put ethics in the centre of your goals, then having open, positive and supportive relationships with the people you encounter will only add to your achievements rather than diminish them.

Finally, it is crucial that if the goals and terms of the expedition change substantially that you inform relevant institutions which have supported your project. This includes funding bodies, but may also be the ministries and local organisations who have given you permission to work, or the sponsoring agencies in your home country.

Conflicts of interest

In your expedition planning and implementation, it is important to acknowledge and remain open about any conflicts of interest. If your work is going to directly benefit you or people close to you, it is crucial that you make these links clear and disclose them to funding bodies and other institutions supporting your work. In the work itself, it is vital to remain impartial and reflexive. The work will diminish in its value if you cannot remain neutral and are unable articulate how you are positioned in relation to the expedition and your participants.

Reflexivity is the process of reflecting on your role in the research process and how elements of yourself as a person influence the work. This *positionality* includes your culture, gender, race, class, personality, and life circumstances (Moss, 2002). In other words, what do you bring to the work and how does that create particular lenses through which you approach the expedition? No one can ever escape these aspects of themselves, so it is not a question of trying to remove bias or somehow becoming someone else, but rather to reflect on how your positionality influences the kind of work you do and the way you interpret your results. It can also help you when coping with difficult cultural circumstances, as it can be a foundation for having a discussion about cultural misunderstandings with people you encounter.

CONCLUSIONS

In conclusion, dealing with ethics for your expedition is a four-step process. First, you need to identify and educate yourself on the appropriate ethical guidelines and codes that are relevant for the core goals of your expedition. Secondly, these will help you to obtain ethical clearance from funding bodies or your institution if required. Even if ethical clearance is not mandatory, writing up an ethical evaluation of the expedition and keeping it on file can cover any legal obligations you may have. Thirdly, you need to educate yourself on the broader context of your expedition and think through any ethical concerns the expedition's travel and encounters with people and non-humans may elicit. You may want to incorporate such issues into your written ethics evaluation. Fourthly, you will need to make ethical evaluations and decisions while in the field that may not be straight-forward. In this final step, it will be crucial to maintain humility and a willingness to change tactics, apologise, or try to un-do any unintentional harm caused.

Overall, ethical codes and guidelines can give you a rough framework for thinking about ethics, but they are not sufficient for making ethical decisions in the field. Each situation is unique and will present challenges that may not necessarily have a clear path to "doing no harm" or helping you decide what is "right". Rather, careful forward planning, educating yourself on the overall context in which you will be operating, and evaluating each situation as it arises will help you to conceptualise and implement your expedition in an ethically sound manner.

IMPLICATIONS FOR PRACTICE

- Do a web search to find some ethical guidelines that are relevant for your expedition's goals. Work through any forms or guidance notes they supply and write out an evaluation of the ethical considerations for your work.

- Consider the ethical evaluation of your work. Does it capture all the ethical issues the expedition itself is likely to bring out? Use the web to search for ethical guidelines that may help you to capture the issues that may be related to the area you will be working, your travelling arrangements or the management of "local" staff. Add these to your write up of ethical considerations for the expedition's goals.

- Once you have done some background research on the area you will visit, take some time to list possible complex ethical issues that might arise. Try to come up with some guidelines and action plans that may help you to make difficult decisions while under pressure in the field.

- In the field, make time to reflect and discuss as a team difficult circumstances that arise. Do you need to create systems or delegate responsibility to individuals in order to keep your expedition operating within the ethical stance it wishes to maintain?

DISCUSSION QUESTIONS

1. Your expedition that wants access to a National Park in a developing nation and has been repeatedly denied permission. Going through all the official channels has yielded no results and, as a team, you have made a clear decision that you

will not provide bribes under any circumstances. At last, you meet someone willing to assist you gaining access to the Park, under the proviso that you help them gain admission to your University for post-graduate study. They are not asking you to go beyond the bounds of normal procedures, but they simply want you to read their application proposal and to provide them with a personal contact. In fact, you know someone who would be ideal as a supervisor. The success of the expedition rests on gaining access to the Park. Is helping someone with their university application, including introducing them to your contact, the same as a bribe? Think through the issues that this example highlights and outline how you might resolve them.

2. A core component of your expedition is documenting the process, and you imagined using photography as a key way to do that. What you had not anticipated was that you would be travelling through land considered sacred for more than half the time and a condition of granting permission to enter this area was that you do not take any photographs. The local people believe that the spirits that live in the land will be disturbed permanently if you do so. As expedition leader you readily agree to this arrangement as travelling through the area is far more important to your goals than photographing it, but on day three of travelling in that area, you discover that one of your expedition members has been taking photographs covertly. How should you handle this situation? Could the problem have been avoided by a more formal arrangement for the storage of cameras while in the sacred area? What are the consequences for trust within the group if you do not handle this situation well? Should you allow the offending team member continue with the expedition? What should you do with the photographs? Should you inform the local people?

3. Your command of the local language is not sufficient to understand all the conversation and you have been relying on getting translations of the transcriptions when you return. Although recording interviews or informal conversations with people uncomfortable with a recorder will make your job much easier, should you record covertly?

4. Members of your team enjoy having a drink to unwind after a long day in the field. However, alcohol abuse is a major problem in this particular area and has a history of leading to a lot of domestic violence. Women have unsuccessfully tried to ban alcohol locally, while the local men are keen to share drinks and chat with the research team. Should you allow the research team to drink?

REFERENCES

Baron, M., Pettit, P., & Slote, M. A. (1997). *Three methods of ethics: Debate*. Oxford, UK: Blackwell.
Hay, I., & Foley, P. (1998). Ethics, geography and responsible citizenship. *Journal of Geography in Higher Education, 22*(2), 169–183.
Held, V. (2006). *The ethics of care: Personal, political, and global*. Oxford, UK: Oxford University Press.
Light, A., & Smith, J. M. (1997). Introduction: Geography, philosophy, and the environment. In A. Light & J. M. Smith (Eds.), *Philsophy and geography I: Space, place, and environmental ethics*. Lanham, MD: Rowman & Littlefield.

Mill, J. S., Bentham, J., & Ryan, A. (1987). *Utilitarianism and other essays.* London: Penguin Books.

Moss, P. (Ed.). (2002). *Feminist geography in practice: Research and methods.* Oxford, UK: Blackwell.

Proctor, J. D. (1998). Geography, paradox and environmental ethics. *Progress in Human Geography, 22*(2), 234–255.

Robson, C. (2002). *Real world research* (2nd ed.). Oxford, UK: Blackwell.

Rose, G. (1993). *Feminist and geography: The limits of geographical knowledge.* Oxford, UK: Blackwell.

Sayer, A., & Storper, M. (1997). Ethics unbound: For a normative turn in social theory. *Environment and Planning D: Society and Space, 15*, 1–17.

Smith, D. M. (1997). Geography and ethics: A moral turn? *Progress in Human Geography, 21*(4), 583–590.

Andrea Nightingale
The University of Edinburgh

SIMON BEAMES AND PETE ALLISON

11. CURRENT ISSUES ON EDUCATIONAL EXPEDITIONS

This final chapter considers some of the current issues in the world of educational expeditions. Many of these issues pertain to expeditions that are taking place in a country foreign to the participants, and may, in some instances, have an obvious UK bias or draw on UK examples. The issues examined in this chapter are volunteer work, cultural sensitivity and environmental responsibility, psychological considerations, regulating practice, conducting research, and accessibility.

VOLUNTEER WORK

Perhaps one of the most inflammatory issues in the current expedition climate surrounds expedition organisations sending young people to developing nations as unskilled labourers. For example, this could entail participants doing jobs such as teaching in primary schools, helping to take zoological surveys, or working in national parks on conservation projects.

Many of these projects may not fall under the strict definition of an expedition, as they may not involve a journey; they may be based in the same place for several weeks at a time – despite being remote and self-sufficient. A number of organisations have elements of expeditions as part of their programmes. For this reason, the issue of unskilled labour is highlighted.

Critics note that Western young people going to developing nations and working may often be considered a form of neo-colonialism (see, in particular, Simpson, 2004). This is so, because there remains an imbalance of power in favour of the participants and the expedition provider. For example, the UK would not tolerate an 18-year-old Ghanaian boy coming to the Southwest of England for six weeks and teaching in a primary school. This lies in contrast to common instances where British youth without appropriate qualifications and with minimal experience find themselves in developing nations, playing prominent roles in the host village's formal education system. While this kind of altruism may be laudable, it may be worth considering that this practice is only made possible by the wide gulf between the resources of the visitor and the host community. This gulf leads to a discussion of a sub-field of experiential education: service learning.

A number of papers have described how service-learning is a branch of experiential education that is gaining increasing prominence in the Western world (Jacoby, 1996; Jakubowski, 2003; Warren & Loeffler, 2000). Jacoby defines service learning as "activities that address human and community needs with

S. K. Beames (ed.), Understanding Educational Expeditions, 113–123.
© 2010 Sense Publishers. All rights reserved.

structured opportunities intentionally designed to promote student learning and development" (p. 5). Typically, service-learning programmes involve living and working in a host community on projects that have been deemed important by the members of that community (Jacoby, 1996; Kendall, 1990).

Meaningful service-learning programmes demand thorough examination, so that they are not merely exercises in being exposed to life in a developing nation, but rather, they engage participants in the daily life of those living in the host country (Levison, 1990). Similarly, service-learning projects ought to ensure that those being served are in control of the services being provided; those being served become more empowered as a result of the project; and those who serve are also learners (Jacoby, 1996; Kendall, 1990). Dickson (1988) recommends educational programmes for young people where the experience is based on "the adventure culminating in service, and the service itself an adventure" (p. 26).

In strict terms, service learning cannot occur without formal reflection (Jacoby, 1996). Service without reflection would likely be regarded by many as volunteerism, as it is not connected to any structured set of learning objectives. We suggest that learning can happen without formal reflective activities (e.g. debriefing in a circle, journal writing). After all, people have learned through experience since the beginning of time. We also recognise that service learning experiences designed to be part of a larger educational programme may need to have specific intended learning outcomes in order to justify their inclusion.

Another feature of service learning is reciprocity, where all parties "are learners and help determine what is to be learned. Both the server and those served teach, and both learn" (Kendall, 1990, p. 22). Furthermore, it is imperative that the members of the host community identify the service tasks and then control the service provided (Jacoby, 1996).

As the above discussion on service learning suggests, expedition providers who are using service as part of their programme can draw from the literature as a means of guiding their own practice. Crucially, expeditions involving volunteer work as a means of learning need to be thoroughly considered and not "added on" in some tokenistic manner. Well-conceptualised and implemented projects have much potential for learning.

CULTURAL SENSITIVITY AND ENVIRONMENTAL RESPONSIBILITY

Along with the issues of health and safety highlighted in the 1990s, expeditions in the new millennium have brought new areas of concern. Critics have identified several potentially problematic aspects of some current practices on youth expeditions, including cultural sensitivity, the use of drugs, and the environmental costs associated with young people travelling outside of their home country (Allison & Higgins, 2002).

First, they were particularly critical of expedition groups that did not show appropriate cultural sensitivity when travelling in developing nations (Allison & Higgins, 2002). Participants who do not cover themselves suitably and wear short and sleeveless tops in Muslim countries are an obvious example. Readers are advised to refer to Nightingale's chapter in this volume for a deeper examination of expedition ethics.

Second, the outcomes of an expedition being so great that they warrant flying a group of 50 young people across the world was highlighted as being questionable (Allison & Higgins, 2002). In a time when air travel is widely accepted as a contributor to global climate change, it seems surprising that so many operators and participants are convinced that they must visit lands far away, despite sometimes knowing little of their home land. This point is contentious and has been responded to by the Young Explorers Trust (YET) who have argued that the benefits outweigh the costs. It seems more than likely that this debate will only gain more energy as issues of climate change continue to receive attention.

In response to some critiques of "universal" outdoor education (i.e. ignoring "place"), there is a movement towards expeditions that take place in the neighbourhoods in which young people live and go to school. *Outdoor Journeys* is an example of a framework designed to allow students of all ages and abilities to generate questions about human history and local ecology (Outdoor Journeys, 2009). Learning about the socio-cultural and geo-physical aspects of landscape involves students taking responsibility for planning their route, managing their primary needs (e.g. food and fluid intake, temperature regulation), and identifying hazards that might be encountered. The aim is for much of the responsibility (and power) to be shifted from the teacher to participants. Ultimately, students should develop the tools necessary to undertake their own developmentally appropriate journeys – either as part of school or not.

Expeditions such as Outdoor Journeys may be attractive to some school boards/local education authorities as they do not require specialist outdoor equipment (e.g. ropes, helmets), expert staff, added transport costs (e.g. hiring buses), and are available to all – regardless of financial means. We want to caution against overseas expeditions and local journeys being dichotomised and set against each other as and "either or". Rather, we see them as being complementary elements of a rich education that all young people are entitled to. Indeed, undertaking self-sufficient journeys early in life may encourage and support children to seek more adventurous travel further afield as they get older.

PSYCHOLOGICAL CONSIDERATIONS

Expeditions present a number of complex and varied challenges that inevitably evoke a range of psychological responses. This aspect of expeditions has received increasing attention and the field of wilderness therapy has sought to address the learning from, and management of, these unavoidable psychological responses. Some responses are considered more positive and associated with learning (e.g. awe and inspiration, considering past experiences, learning how to interact with others), while others have more negative connotations (e.g. home sickness, psychosocial challenges, eating disorders). Furthermore, the responses to such experiences occur not only during expeditions, but also afterwards, when participants return to their home community. Broadly speaking, there are three psychological areas to consider.

The first area is learning in a safe (physical and emotional) environment. Taking people on expeditions is often motivated, to some extent, by trying to trigger some kind of psychological or emotional response to various aspects of the experience. For some this may be about developing themselves, understanding themselves and others, and as an opportunity to reflect on their lives, behaviours, and relationships - past, present, and future. For others, the expedition may be a time when reflection brings to the fore difficult issues that may have been previously suppressed, such as confidence, dysfunctional relationships, existential challenges, and sense of life-direction. Clearly, leaders need to be appropriately prepared to deal with these and related issues. To this end, planning prior to an expedition, including reviewing applications and holding interviews, gaining medical information, writing clear marketing material, and conducting thorough training weekends are crucial in minimising psychological difficulties that will undoubtedly arise.

Second, post-expedition responses are often difficult to gauge, and until relatively recently, had not been studied. The phenomenon can be understood as similar to the blues when returning from holiday or to a process of mourning (e.g. for the wilderness, for friends, for simplicity of expedition life). For many young people, going on an expedition for the first time can be life-changing; it is often the first visit to a far off place, to the wilderness, and of experiencing cultures very different from their own. As such, returning to everyday life (school, home, university, employment) is often rather awkward. Indeed, it is common for people to report difficulties sleeping inside, making decisions about what to eat, amazement at the number of people they meet and missing the intimacy of the relationships experienced on the expedition. Allison (1999; 2000; 2005) studied expeditions and discovered this phenomenon to be common among the majority of participants. He comments,

> It seems reasonable to conclude that some adjustment post–expedition might be expected for the majority of people. If there were no signs of some type of post–expedition adjustment then one could question if there had been any changes or examination of values during the expedition experience. (Allison, 2005, p. 23).

The third psychological area that expedition leaders need to deal with concerns managing threats to the learning environment. When people do experience some of the challenges outlined above, such as adjustment problems (to and from the expedition), illness/accidents, crises (emotional and otherwise), it is vital that leaders have the skills to recognise them, decide on a course of action, manage and remedy them, and avoid them occurring again - unless these problems are deemed to be desirable (rarely the case). These processes are explored in more detail by Berman and Davis-Berman (2002) and Berman, Davis-Berman, and Gillen (1998).

Space does not permit a detailed exploration of this aspect of expeditions, but those who are interested are advised to read Davis-Berman and Berman (2008) and the classic study in this area by Kaplan and Talbot (1983).

REGULATING PRACTICE IN THE UK AND BEYOND

Most of the expeditions taking place in the UK that involve participants under the age of 18 years old are regulated by the Adventure Activities Licensing Service (AALS), which was developed following a kayaking tragedy in 1993 and the subsequent Young Persons Safety Act (1995). The word "most" is used deliberately, as expeditions that are in non-technical terrain and have rapid access to roads may not be classified as licensable by AALS (AALS, n.d.). For example, an expedition in a flat, forested area that is not far from a road may not require the provider to be licensed by AALS. Naturally, there are elements of duty of care and basic health and safety that need to be adhered to, but there is no need for the leader to have an outdoor qualification, such as the Mountain Leader award.

If the expedition involves travelling in more remote and demanding country (usually higher hills or on the water), then by law the activity is licensable under AALS. This means that (among other things) AALS ensures that the activity provider has competent staff and is using properly maintained safety equipment. It is important to note a crucial exception to AALS regulations: expeditions for those under the age of 18 in Britain are not licensable under AALS, if the expedition leader is not being paid (e.g. a teacher leading an expedition with student participants) (AALS, n.d.). Once the expedition leaves the United Kingdom, things become less clear, as there is no statutory obligation for providers to operate at a given standard or for leaders to be qualified.

However, since 1972 the Young Explorers Trust (YET), which is a UK independent educational charity, has approved expeditions through its national evaluation system. This process was designed and developed as a means of supporting expedition organisers and leaders, as well as improving the quality of provision while giving expeditions "YET approved" status. YET also offer a small grant system to support expeditions they approve and which are in need of financial support. In 2008 the YET screening process incorporated British Standard 8848 to become the *YET evaluation process*.

British Standards 8848, which was published in 2007 (and reviewed and updated in 2009), is the closest the sector has come to regulating the practice of overseas ventures. The Standard is not limited to expeditions, but rather, covers any kind of visit, trip, or fieldwork outside of the UK (BS 8848, 2007). 8848's principal goal is to minimise injuries and illness during these ventures. The onus to follow the practices outlined in the Standard is placed squarely on the "venture provider". Third party employees (such as bus drivers or mountaineering instructors) may be used by the venture provider as long as 8848's specifications are being followed. At the time of writing, expedition companies are not required to adhere to 8848, but presumably gain credibility in the eyes of the public if they do.

All of the above outlined systems (AALS, YET, and BS 8848) are concerned with a systems approach and accrediting organisations rather than certifying individuals. This approach has been developed in response to an increasing number of overseas expeditions taking place in a wide range of environments with a broad spectrum of aims. In these varying circumstances, specifying individual leader certifications may be too complex to manage. As an example, compare the leadership skills that are needed for a small school group going on a two week expedition from the UK to the Swiss Alps, with the skills needed for a three month expedition for individuals from across the UK who are travelling to Kenya to kayak, undertake some service learning projects, and visit some game reserves. To address such differences the evaluation system for BS 8848 which is administered through the YET, offers a flexible approach that considers the specific expedition aims, location and context in a descriptive rather than prescriptive manner. The approach encourages organisations and individuals to focus on managing the plethora of situations they may encounter on expeditions and not create cumbersome paperwork.

In this section we have specifically focused on the UK context in order to provide some depth and context to the issue of regulating practice. Other countries are currently facing similar issues which can not all be detailed in the space available.

CONDUCTING EXPEDITION RESEARCH

Research can be undertaken on expeditions in two broad categories: first, research about the environment that is being visited (e.g. geology or tourism), and second, participants and leaders being studied as a means of understanding the influences and processes occurring during and after an expedition. In this section we focus on the second of these two categories. Undertaking empirical research on expeditions can present challenges beyond those normally associated with ethnographic methodologies. It is relatively straight-forward to collect data after the experience - through questionnaires and interviews, for example. Whether one is collecting data as an expedition leader, a participant, or as a specialist researcher, there are pros and cons to actually being on an expedition and researching the other people on the expedition. There is no right solution, but rather the most appropriate, depending on the specific aims of the research, the questions being asked and the epistemological preferences of the researcher(s). Therefore, although possible approaches are outlined in countless texts on research methodologies, the onus is on the researcher to choose a methodology that will most effectively answer the research question.

Actually being on the expedition that one is investigating is a privilege that must not abused. Having such intimate and constant access to (normally) willing participants is unusual in the world of research (but common in anthropological studies). On expedition, going to the toilet is probably the only thing that researchers may not witness, as everything else – the banal and the exciting – is normally on display. As Potter's (1998) examination of the human dimensions of expeditions informs us: "during expeditions people live in close quarters 24 hours a day and generally lose their taken for granted privacies…options to check out from the group, sometimes even briefly, are greatly reduced and frequently impossible" (p. 256). This kind of access for the researcher can bring a familiarity – and consequent level of understanding – that offers ethnographic approaches (e.g. living with the expedition) much credibility.

As a researcher on the expedition, one cannot help but somehow influence people's interactions and behaviours. The degree to which one is participating in expedition life, as well as the overtness of one's data collection methods, need to be carefully considered. For example, if one does not fully participate in expedition life (which is difficult to do in itself) but is sitting nearby, taking notes or asking people to complete questionnaires at regular intervals, then this process can impact on individuals in numerous ways. First, members may alter their behaviours if they know they are being watched (see the Hawthorne Effect) and second, they may answer questionnaires (and similar "instruments") in order to present themselves in a certain way (e.g. with the aim of increasing their social "currency"). On the other hand, if one fully participates in expedition life (e.g. participant observation – see Spradley, 1980) and is never seen to be formally interviewing anyone or taking notes, then one may gain a deeper understanding of what people think and do – which is probably what the researcher is most curious about. The concerns in this instance are that a) the researchers are such a part of expedition life that they overly influence the group, and b) they lose their ability to find a balanced perspective on the group and their role within it. Subjectivity in the research process can be seen as a strength in this example, but if the study is to remain an investigation about individuals and the group (apart from the researcher), then some distance needs to be maintained. Again, there is no "one solution" – only the most appropriate for the circumstances with reference to the issues being explored by the researcher.

Another important aspect of collecting data on expeditions is the meteorological conditions. For example, pouring rain and a howling gale at the campsite may not be the most suitable conditions for conducting a recorded interview with a participant, as he or she may not be fully focused on the discussion. Certainly, with a nod to Maslow (1968) it is worth considering the degree to which one's primary needs (e.g. food, shelter, warmth) are taken care of, and how this may affect the state of the interviewee. On the contrary, a researcher who is hoping to capture a deeper essence of "the moment" may choose to put microphones in front of participants' faces precisely during stressful or uncomfortable occasions. Some parts of an expedition may be so stressful that it would simply be unfeasible to pursue any kind of data collection. Take, for instance, wanting to ask someone about how they are feeling while descending a mountain ridge during a blizzard, or while rushing to take down a sail during storm at sea. This raises further issues regarding researchers' assumptions of when people may be more or less stressed. For some, descending a mountain ridge may be stressful, while for others making a meal at camp may be challenging. Thus, the timing of such approaches to research will inevitably be better for some participants than others.

In these scenarios, it may be more useful to use fieldnotes (see for example Emerson, Fretz, and Shaw, 1995). This might involve pulling out a small notebook once off the above-mentioned hypothetical ridge and trying to recount a particularly meaningful item that was said or observed. Informal conversations may also serve as rich data. For example, after the storm at sea has passed, there may be insightful comments offered by participants over a cup of tea in the galley. Here again, the small notebook and pencil become valuable items in the researcher's tool box. The point of these examples has been to emphasise that whatever the decision of the researcher, they need to be considered on both logistical and ethical grounds.

Alternative approaches to those already outlined might involve asking those involved in expeditions to write about their experiences at a time at which they feel ready. Further forms of data may also prove to be fruitful, such as artwork, personal journals, poetry and other creative outlets that are often present on expeditions.

Another area worthy of mention in this section is the limitations of ac/dc power availability in the field. A recent examination of this challenge is offered by Stonehouse (2007), who has used a solar panel to recharge his iPod (with microphone attachment for interviews) in the field. He also recommends using a small word-processing keyboard for typing daily field notes. Having notes that can be easily converted into MS Word has to be considered against carrying the added weight of the keyboard. Certainly, the advent of digital recorders for interviews, focus groups, and field notes has greatly facilitated researchers' ability to return from expedition with many hours of data that takes up little space and is increasingly easy to analyse with modern qualitative data software.

In this section we have noted a few of the issues associated with data collection undertaken during expeditions. It is worth noting three final points. First, the little work that has been conducted in this area has been primarily empirical research. There are extensive opportunities for philosophical exploration of educational expeditions. Second, little, if any, research has focused on the learning of all involved in an expedition (such as leaders, assistant leaders, members of local communities visited, organisations) but has rather focused on the learning of the young people or participants involved. Third, there is growing pressure for outcome focused research to "prove" the value of expeditions empirically. Methodologically this is challenging and has met with little success (Allison & Pomeroy, 2000; Thomas & Pring, 2004).

ACCESSIBILITY

It is not particularly contentious to point out that there are inequalities between different people's access to resources in society. These resources might be such things as food, education, medical help, and property.

Historically, the world of educational expeditions has been dominated by rich white people (e.g. early expeditions run by the Public Schools Exploring Society). The period from the mid-1970s to the mid-1980s saw the British overseas youth expedition transform from a product exclusively for the socio-economically privileged to one catering to a "much larger range of children of varying social backgrounds and academic abilities" (Grey, 1984, p. 17). An example of these programmes is Kennedy's (1984; 1992) overland expeditions to the Sahara desert with inner city youth from Liverpool. Current initiatives such as the *Next Generation* scheme offered by the British Schools Exploring Society are examples of promoting equality of opportunity.

In the UK today, although more opportunities exist for marginalised people to take part in expeditions – whether as part of the Duke of Edinburgh scheme or on a summer-long mission to the arctic – a fundamental discrepancy between the demographics of those who go on expeditions and those who do not, appears to remain.

In Scotland, where students from the bottom 20% of the socio-economic spectrum are seven times more likely to be excluded from school than those in the top 20% (Scottish Government, 2009), one can reasonably speculate that expedition opportunities for the former will come from a youth-at-risk programme of some sort. Conversely, those within the top 20% wanting to go on an expedition will more usually rely on their parents paying substantial amounts of money. If participants' parents do not pay directly, there is anecdotal evidence suggesting that money may often be raised with the help of their parents' social and business networks.

Beyond financial matters, it is quite likely that in social networks characterised by chronic low income, young people are not interested in going on an expedition, as there is little history of any family member or friend so doing. Equally, teenagers attending an independent school with a strong tradition of expeditioning, may feel stigmatised if they do not take a given expedition opportunity. It is conceivable to suggest that by choosing to participate in an expedition, they are merely "going with the flow" and following dominant social forces.

The implication for practitioners in all countries and cultures is that if the outcomes of an expedition are desirable for all young people - as a means to increase overall personal growth and well being - then surely these kinds of experiences ought to be available to all, irrespective of financial power, physical ability, sex, gender, religion, or ethnicity.

FINAL THOUGHTS

In 2008, a "knowledge exchange" conference was organised in Edinburgh, as a means to discuss and share information about overseas expeditions. The conference was successful in bringing together expedition providers, policy makers, and academics, so they could discuss topical issues. As with any kind of practice within any kind of sector, some issues may unite or polarise those involved. This chapter acknowledges that there are countless issues within the field of educational expeditions. In particular, there are issues that will have much more personal and cultural relevance to each reader than the ones briefly outlined above. Undoubtedly, future work will expand upon some of the issues presented and we anticipate that they will appear as chapters in future editions of this book.

Ultimately, it is not so much the issues themselves that we hope readers will concentrate on, but rather how these issues are considered. Our aim has been to illustrate how we need to challenge taken-for-granted assumptions about our practice in terms of equity and power between expedition providers, researchers, participants, and the people who live on the land through which our journeys travel.

REFERENCES

AALS. (n.d.). *The scope of the regulations*. Adventurous Activities Licensing Service. Retrieved January 13, 2009, from http://www.aals.org.uk/faqs.html#scope

Allison, P., & Higgins, P. (2002). Ethical adventures: Can we justify overseas youth expeditions in the name of education? *Australian Journal of Outdoor Education, 6*(2), 22–26.

Allison, P., & Pomeroy, E. (2000). How shall we 'know?': Epistemological concerns in research in experiential education. *Journal of Experiential Education, 23*(2), 91–97.

Allison, P. (1999). Post residential syndrome—Research from the ground up. In M. White (Ed.), *Experiencing the difference: Conference report* (pp. 74–76). Cumbria: Brathay Hall Trust.

Allison, P. (2000). *Research from the ground up: Post expedition adjustment*. Cumbria: Brathay Hall Trust.

Allison, P. (2005). *Post–expedition adjustment: What empirical data suggest?* Estes Park, CO: WEA Conference Proceedings.

Berman, D., & Davis-Berman, J. (2002). An integrated approach to crisis management in wilderness settings. *Journal of Adventure Education and Outdoor Learning, 2*(1), 9–17.

Berman, D., David-Berman, J., & Gillen, M. (1998). Behavioural and emotional crisis management in adventure education. *Journal of Experiential Education, 21*, 96–101.

British Standards 8848. (2007). *Specification for the provision of visits, fieldwork, expeditions, and adventurous activities, outside the United Kingdom*. London: BSI.

David-Berman, J., & Berman, D. (2008). *The promise of wilderness therapy*. Boulder, CO: Association for Experiential Education.

Dickson, A. (1988). Return from the mountain. *Horizons, 5*(3), 20–26.

Emerson, R. M., Fretz, R. I., & Shaw, L. L. (1995). *Writing ethnographic fieldnotes*. Chicago: University of Chicago Press.

Grey, T. (1984). The expedition experience. *Adventure Education,* March/April, 17–18.

Jacoby, B. (1996). Service learning in today's higher education. In B. Jacoby (Ed.), *Service learning in higher education: Concepts and practices* (pp. 3–25). San Francisco: Jossey-Bass.

Jakubowski, L. M. (2003). Beyond book learning: Cultivating the pedagogy of experience through field trips. *Journal of Experiential Education, 26*(1), 24–33.

Kaplan, S., & Talbot, J. F. (1983). Psychological benefits of a wilderness experience. In I. Altman & J. Wohlwill (Eds.), *Human behaviour and environment: Advances in theory and research* (pp. 163–205). New York: Plenum Press.

Kendall, J. C. (1990). Combining service and learning: An introduction. In J. C. Kendall & Associates (Eds.), *Combining service and learning: A resource book for community and public service* (Vol. 1, pp. 1–33). Raleigh, NC: National Society for Internships and Experiential Education.

Kennedy, A. (1984, March/April). Liverpool schoolboys Sahara expedition. *Adventure Education,* 19–20.

Kennedy, A. (1992). *The expedition experience as a vehicle for change in the inner city*. Penrith, NSW: Adventure Education.

Levison, L. M. (1990). Choose engagement over exposure. In J. C. Kendall & Associates (Eds.), *Combining service and learning: A resource book for community and public service* (Vol. 1, pp. 68–75). Raleigh, NC: National Society for Internships and Experiential Education.

Maslow, A. H. (1968). Some educational implications of humanistic psychologies. *Harvard Educational Review, 38*(4), 685–696.

Outdoor Journeys. (2009). *What is outdoor journeys?* Retrieved January 19, 2009, from http://www.outdoorjourneys.org.uk/Outdoor_Journeys/Home.html

Potter, T. G. (1998). *Human dimensions of expeditions: Deeply rooted, branching out*. Paper presented at the 1997 Association for Experiential Education International Conference, Ashville, North Carolina. ED414123

Scottish Government. (2009). *Exclusions from schools 2007/2008*. Statistics Publication Notice: Education Series, ISSN 1479-7569. Retrieved June 16, 2009, from http://www.scotland.gov.uk/Publications/2009/01/23135939/35

Simpson, K. (2004). 'Doing development': The gap year, volunteer-tourists and a popular practice of development. *Journal of International Development, 16*(5), 681–692.

Spradley, J. P. (1980). *Participant observation*. London: Thomson Learning.

Stonehouse, P. (2007). Recording in the wild: A reflection on research technology needs on an expedition. *Australian Journal of Outdoor Education, 11*(1), 47–49.

Thomas, G., & Pring, R. (Eds.). (2004). *Evidence-based practice in education*. Maidenhead, UK: Oxford University Press.

Warren, K., & Loeffler, T. A. (2000). Setting a place at the table: Social justice research in outdoor experiential education. *Journal of Experiential Education, 23*(2), 85–90.

The authors would like to thank Dene Berman, Peter Harvey, and Nigel Harling for their helpful comments on earlier versions of this chapter.

Simon Beames and Pete Allison
The University of Edinburgh

CPSIA information can be obtained at www.ICGtesting.com
Printed in the USA
BVOW06s1957251015

424002BV00003B/52/P